DK

What if...

→ YOU ←

DIDN'T

make

SNOT?

Written by **EMMA YOUNG**

Illustrated by **SUPER FREAK**

CONTENTS

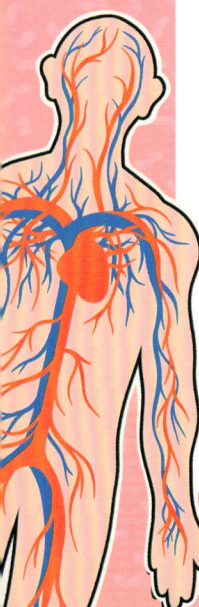

Warning: This book discusses some funny and outrageous questions around the human body. These are not experiments to be tried out, and the publisher cannot accept any liability for any injury or damage should a reader attempt to do so.

What if you were totally covered in hair?

Imagine having thick hair all over your body, like a Highland cow. You'd never hear, "Don't forget your coat!", again. And you wouldn't ever get told off for getting your clothes filthy – because you wouldn't need any! But would life be different in other ways, too?

Hair hotspots

You already have a few patches of thicker hair, but what are they actually for? Your hairiest bits are your:

👑 **Head** – you have about 100,000 head hairs. They keep your head warm in the cold and protect it from the heat of the sun.

👑 **Eyelashes** – you have about 420 eyelash hairs. One of their jobs is to keep nasty dust out of your eyes.

👑 **Eyebrows** – you have about 600 eyebrow hairs. They also trap dust, and sweat.

Tiny mites can live in your eyelashes.

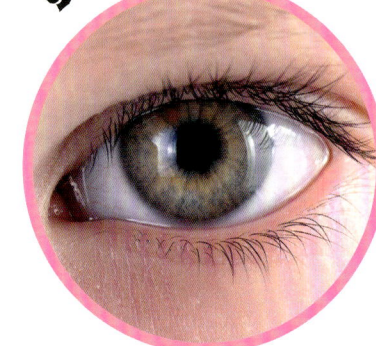

4

Amazing eyebrows

Eyebrows have other uses, apart from trapping dust. They help us to signal how we're feeling to other people. When we're surprised, our eyebrows shoot up. When we're cross, they squeeze together. They're also surprisingly useful for helping us to recognize each other.

Your only completely hairless bits are the palms of your hands and the soles of your feet.

All the hair you can see above your skin's surface is dead (that's why it doesn't hurt when it's cut).

Hair holes

Your hairs grow out of little holes in your skin, called hair follicles. You have about five million hair follicles, spread almost all over your body. That's actually about the same number as for a chimp, it's just that your hair is MUCH thinner than a chimp's. It's thought that our move to wispy hair helped our ancient ancestors stay cool as they left forests to live in more open, hotter areas.

Hairs grow from a root at their base.

Head lice can live in your hair and suck your blood.

The answer?

In fact, you are already almost completely covered in hair. But if all that hair was thick, you couldn't use your eyebrows to signal how you're feeling. You might also struggle to recognize your friends. And you could easily overheat. You'd also get through a lot more shampoo!

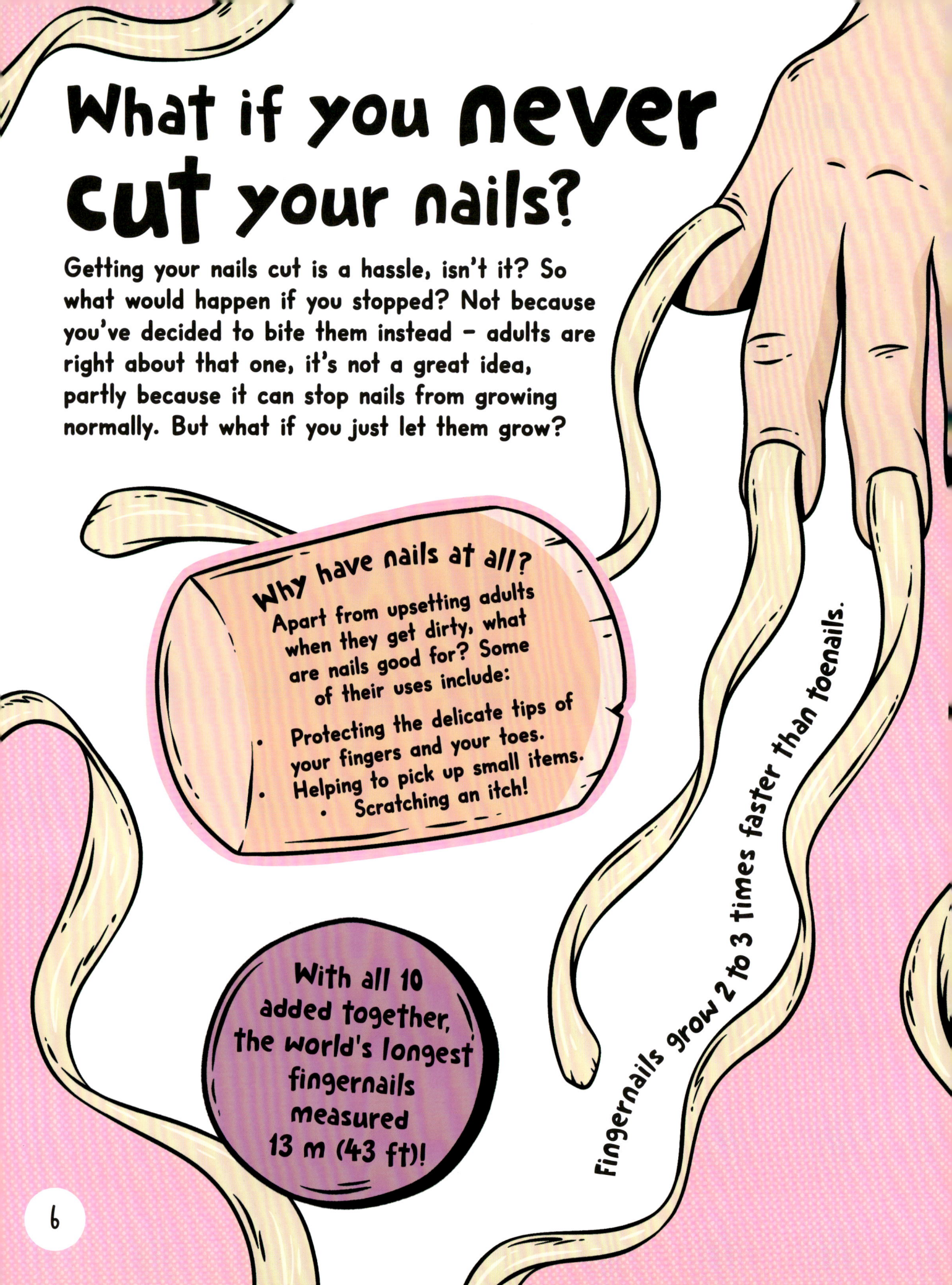

What if you never cut your nails?

Getting your nails cut is a hassle, isn't it? So what would happen if you stopped? Not because you've decided to bite them instead – adults are right about that one, it's not a great idea, partly because it can stop nails from growing normally. But what if you just let them grow?

Why have nails at all?

Apart from upsetting adults when they get dirty, what are nails good for? Some of their uses include:

- Protecting the delicate tips of your fingers and your toes.
- Helping to pick up small items.
- Scratching an itch!

With all 10 added together, the world's longest fingernails measured 13 m (43 ft)!

Fingernails grow 2 to 3 times faster than toenails.

Nails and claws

Your nails are mostly made up of a tough substance called keratin (said KEH-ra-tin). So are a cat's claws, an eagle's talons, and the outer bits of a horse's hooves. You'll also find keratin in your hair, and even the top layer of your skin. Most animals' nails wear down through use, they don't have to cut them.

Nail that sticks out at the end dries and turns white.

This bit is attached to the skin beneath.

New nail forms here.

Always growing

Like your hair, your nails grow from the bottom, not the top. Their roots are buried under the skin right at the base of your nails. As new nail forms there, it pushes the older bit out. This older part gets flatter and harder – and your nail gets longer. Your lazy hair stops growing after a while, and falls out, but your nails don't. If you don't cut them – and they don't break – they'll keep on getting longer, and longer, and longer!

The answer?

If you never cut your nails, they would just keep on growing. But if you want to beat the world record for the longest fingernails that won't be easy. Each one would need to be about as long as you are tall right now, which might make it hard to get dressed, or write, or do lots of things!

7

What if you could take off YOUR SKIN?

If you're thinking, "Not a good idea", you'd be right. If you looked in the mirror, you'd look completely different – you'd see shiny strips of muscle, and bone, and the hard bits of your nose. The good news is that nothing would fall out – your organs, muscles, and so on would all stay where they are. But that's DEFINITELY where the good news ends...

Keeping things OUT

The skin you can see is just the top layer. It's very thin, but it's made of minute blocks of the same tough stuff as your nails. Its job is to stop things such as germs, water, and dirt from getting inside you. If you lost this layer, rain would soak right in.

A lot of house dust is dead skin. In your life, you'll shed 35 kg (77 lb) of it!

Keeping things IN

You can probably see some veins through your skin. These veins are attached to the underside of your skin and are connected to bigger, deeper veins. If you took off your skin, the veins you can see would be ripped off those bigger, deeper veins, and your blood would pour out everywhere!

Your thinnest skin is on your eyelids.

Under the surface

Your skin has three layers. The top layer is a barrier. The middle layer has lots of jobs – it is home to: cells that let you feel touch, cells that fight germs, the roots of your hairs, blood vessels, and glands that make sweat. The bottom layer is mostly fat. This layer is thin on your fingers, but thicker on your tummy. Fat keeps you warm and makes an important vitamin, called vitamin D.

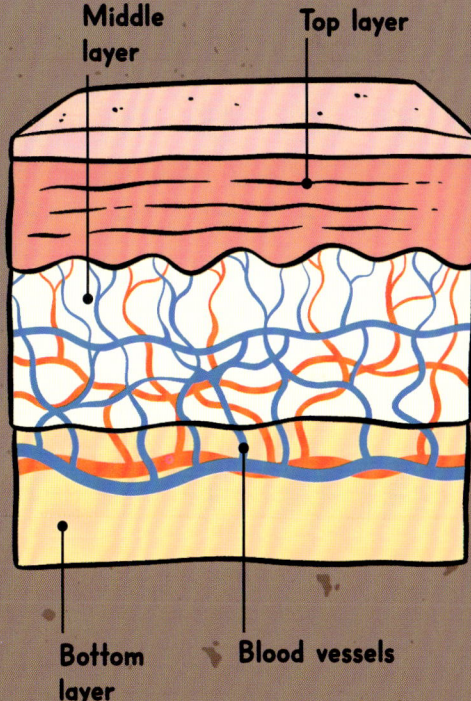

Middle layer

Top layer

Bottom layer

Blood vessels

The answer?

You would lose your heat and your sense of touch immediately. And germs would easily get inside you. But most importantly, your blood would pour out. Yes, you would die!

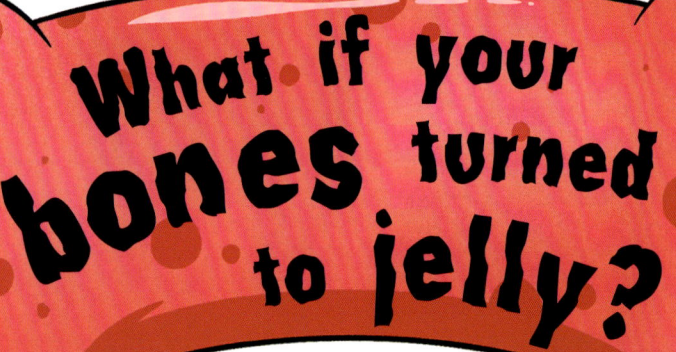

What if your bones turned to jelly?

Eww. Just imagine if the bones in your arms, your legs, your spine, even your head, all turned to wobbly jelly... you don't need me to tell you that you'd be in big trouble. But you might be surprised by exactly which kinds of trouble!

Our smallest bone, in the ear, is the size of a grain of rice!

Bones might look dead but are very much alive!

Tough bones

Your bones have different parts to help them do their job. They have:

A hard, tough outer layer. This gives them strength and means they don't break at every knock.

A core that's full of tiny holes. These holes let blood flow through the bone, and mean that your skeleton is light enough for you to lug around.

Bone nursery

Inside most big bones, you'll find soft, fatty stuff. This is called "bone marrow", and it has a really important job – it makes baby cells that develop into: red blood cells (which carry vital oxygen around your body), white blood cells (which fight infections), and platelets (which help to stop cuts from bleeding).

Most broken bones heal in just 6-8 weeks.

There are 22 bones in the skull.

The ribcage protects your heart and lungs.

Each foot contains 26 bones.

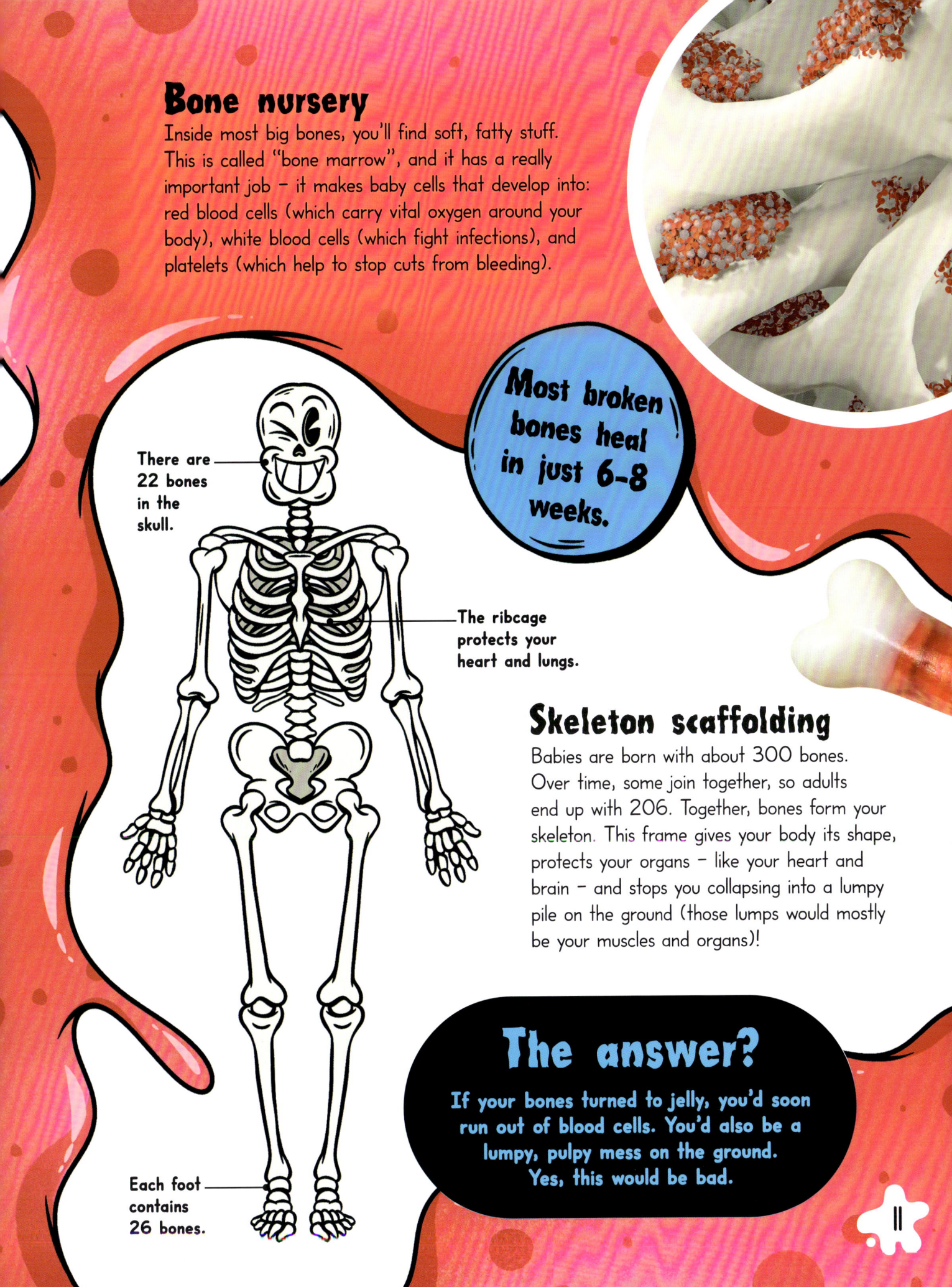

Skeleton scaffolding

Babies are born with about 300 bones. Over time, some join together, so adults end up with 206. Together, bones form your skeleton. This frame gives your body its shape, protects your organs – like your heart and brain – and stops you collapsing into a lumpy pile on the ground (those lumps would mostly be your muscles and organs)!

The answer?

If your bones turned to jelly, you'd soon run out of blood cells. You'd also be a lumpy, pulpy mess on the ground. Yes, this would be bad.

What if you didn't have knees?

How many times have you fallen over and scraped your knees? Maybe it would be better not to have them? No one could blame you for thinking that. But those knobbly knees can be quite useful. Especially when it comes to outdoor games!

Ostriches have two kneecaps on each leg!

You kneed them!

There are lots of different things you couldn't do if you didn't have knees. If you couldn't bend your legs, you couldn't:

- Kick a football
- Ride a bike
- Jump on a trampoline
- Scale a climbing frame
- Sit down on a sofa – not without throwing yourself backwards and hoping for the best!

Curl and bend

A place where two bones meet is called a joint. There are lots of joints between the bones in your spine, which runs down your back. This means you can curl your back to touch your toes or for a forward roll. Other joints include your shoulders, elbows, ankles – and your knees. Without elbows, you couldn't bend your arms. Without knees, you couldn't bend your legs.

Inside your knee

The knee is where your thigh bone (the femur) connects to your shin bone (the tibia). The kneecap (patella) sits above the knee joint. This is the bit of bone that gets bashed when you fall on your knees. That is one of its main jobs, though – to protect the joint. It also helps you to bend and straighten your leg. Tough, rope-like structures called ligaments hold the bones in a joint together.

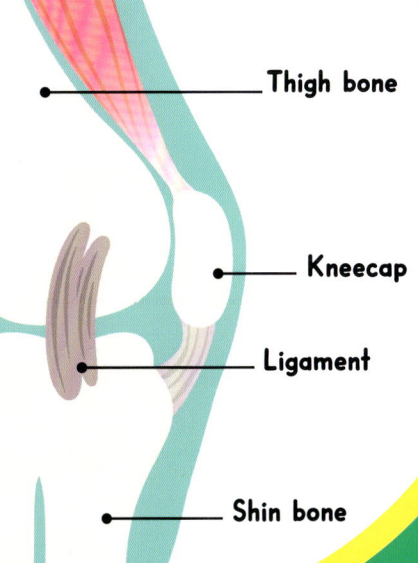

Thigh bone

Kneecap

Ligament

Shin bone

The answer?

If you didn't have knees, you couldn't scrape them. But you couldn't do all kinds of fun everyday activities, either. Better to keep them!

What if you had teeth like a hippo?

Hippos have an impressive set of jaws. Who wouldn't want those massive, pointy front teeth? Well, you might not. While these gnashers would win you first prize in every monster look-alike competition, they're pretty useless when it comes to eating...

Huge hippo canine teeth are also known as tusks.

Tremendous Teeth

A hippo's largest teeth are called canines. You have canines, too. They're great for tearing into stuff – like a sandwich, if you're you, or another hippo, if you're a hippo. For hippos, their canines are mostly used for fighting, rather than eating. The hippo's main food is grass and as any cow will tell you, gigantic pointy teeth aren't required.

Chew and chomp

Most animals that munch on grass move their jaws from side to side while they're eating. This lets them grind that tough grass between their molars, which are flatter teeth at the back of the mouth. You have molars. And so do hippos, but when they shut their mouths, their huge canines get in the way and mean they can only chew up and down!

Incisors: These are good for cutting into, and biting off, bits of food.

Canines: These are good for tearing up food.

Molars: These are for crushing and grinding.

Premolars: A bit like a cross between canines and molars, these are for both tearing and grinding.

Upper jaw

Lower jaw

Baby teeth

Adult teeth

Types of Teeth

Children have 20 small baby teeth. They usually start falling out around the age of six. Gradually, they're replaced with bigger, permanent teeth. Adults have an extra twelve teeth, too, making 32 in total. As well as canines and molars, there are two other types of teeth, called incisors and premolars. Each type has a different job.

Tooth enamel (the white bit) is the hardest material in your body.

The answer?

You really don't want teeth like a hippo. It's surprising that they manage to eat much at all!

15

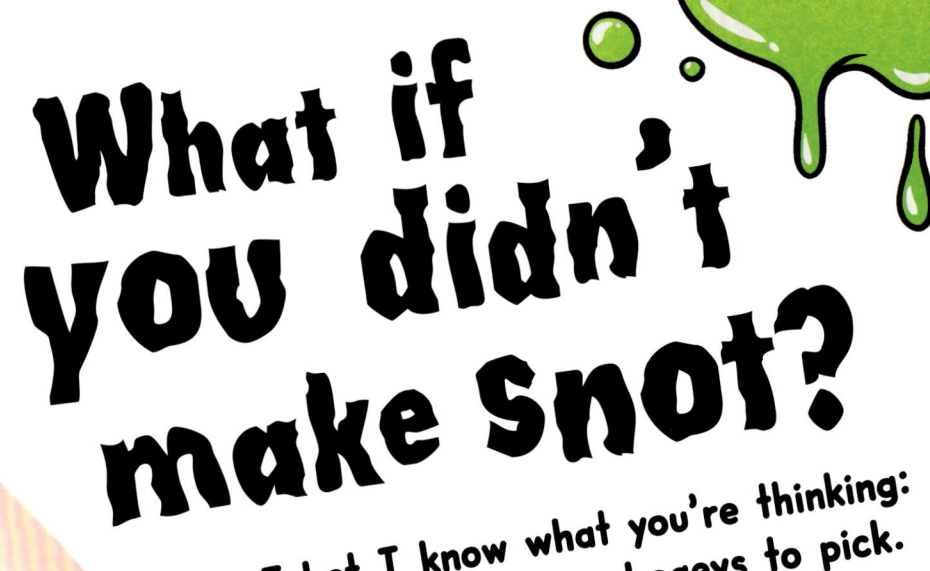

What if you didn't make snot?

I bet I know what you're thinking: no snot means no bogeys to pick. But trust me, if you didn't make snot, this would be the least of your worries. Though snot might seem like useless slime, it has a list of jobs that makes most of us look extremely lazy...

Every day you produce a litre (about four tall glasses) of snot.

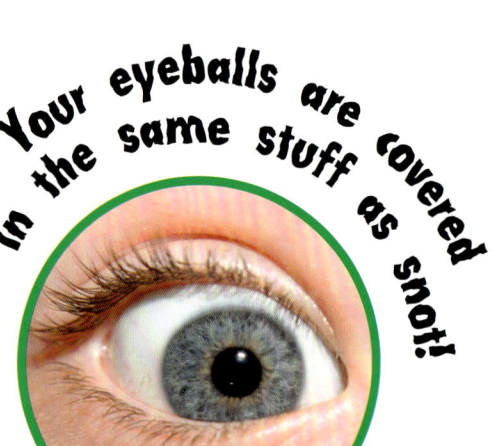

Your eyeballs are covered in the same stuff as snot!

16

Useful mucus

Snot is also called "mucus". It's mostly water, plus a few other chemicals. The gloopy mucus does some very important things:

* It traps dirt, dust, and bacteria.

* It keeps the delicate lining of your nostrils nice and moist.

* It contains germ-killing agents that stop you getting ill.

Picky eater...

Though it might be tempting to pick out bogeys, that snot is likely to be packed with bacteria. These bacteria will get all over your finger and under your nail, and then onto whatever you pick up to eat, so blow bogeys into a tissue instead.

Bacteria can be breathed in through the nose.

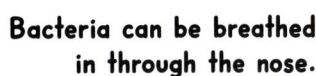

Snot swallower

Infections and allergies can make snot thick. Usually, though, it's thin and clear. Any germs you breathe in stick to it and are swept into the back of your throat for you to swallow away — yes, you are a snot-swallower, as is your teacher! If your nose mucus starts to dry out before it can get pushed towards your throat, it can get lodged there. This is the first stage of the formation of a crusty bogey.

They are trapped by the sticky snot.

Then the bacteria are swallowed safely away.

The answer?

Slimy snot is crucial for good health. If you didn't make it, your nose would dry out. Your nose would soon get sore and you'd start having nosebleeds. Also, you'd get more infections, so you'd be sicker.

17

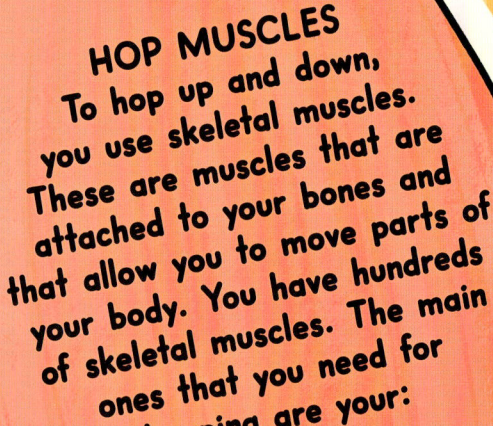

HOP MUSCLES

To hop up and down, you use skeletal muscles. These are muscles that are attached to your bones and that allow you to move parts of your body. You have hundreds of skeletal muscles. The main ones that you need for hopping are your:

H **Calves** – At the back of your lower legs.

H **Hamstrings** – Which run down the back of your thighs.

H **Quadriceps** – At the front of your thighs.

H **Glutes** – Your butt (buttock) muscles.

What if you started hopping everywhere?

We walk a lot. So why not try something else? Rabbits hop. Kangaroos hop. Hopping mice even get their name from their style of getting from A to B. These animals take their springy, bouncy leaps using both legs at the same time. For you, though, it'll probably be easier to hop on one...

Hopping practice

If you started to hop everywhere, and so used your hopping muscles a lot, they'd gradually get bigger and be able to store more energy. Over time, you'd be able to hop for longer and longer before they ran out of that energy, and felt tired.

Your buttocks are the **biggest** muscles in your body.

To bend your knee, your hamstrings, at the back of your thigh, tighten...

...and your quadriceps, at the front, relax.

HOW TO HOP

Muscles are made up of lots of tiny stretchy fibres. When you decide to take a hopping step, your brain sends patterns of signals to the necessary muscles. Some mean: "Tighten!". Others mean: "Relax!". When a muscle tightens, it gets shorter and pulls on the bone that it's attached to – and the bone moves. When it relaxes, it stops pulling on the bone. The bone can then be pulled in the opposite direction by another muscle.

The answer?

You could start hopping everywhere. But it'll take a while for all your hopping muscles to get strong enough to carry you very far. And you will end up with lopsided legs. The hopping one will develop huge, strong muscles. The muscles on the other will shrink!

19

What if you spent your life upside down?

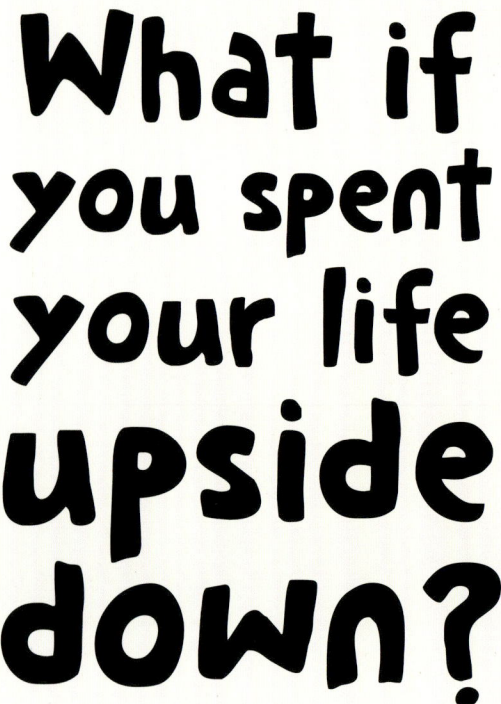

Imagine seeing everything the wrong way up!

Do you love hanging from your knees on a climbing frame? Or rollercoaster loop-the-loops? Then how about spending your entire life the other way up? Well – spoiler alert – there'd be some pretty big upside-down-sides...

Rollercoaster ride

In 2024, a ride at an American amusement park stopped suddenly and 32 people were stranded upside down for about nine minutes. For healthy people, this shouldn't cause any long-term problems. However, it soons starts to become dangerous.

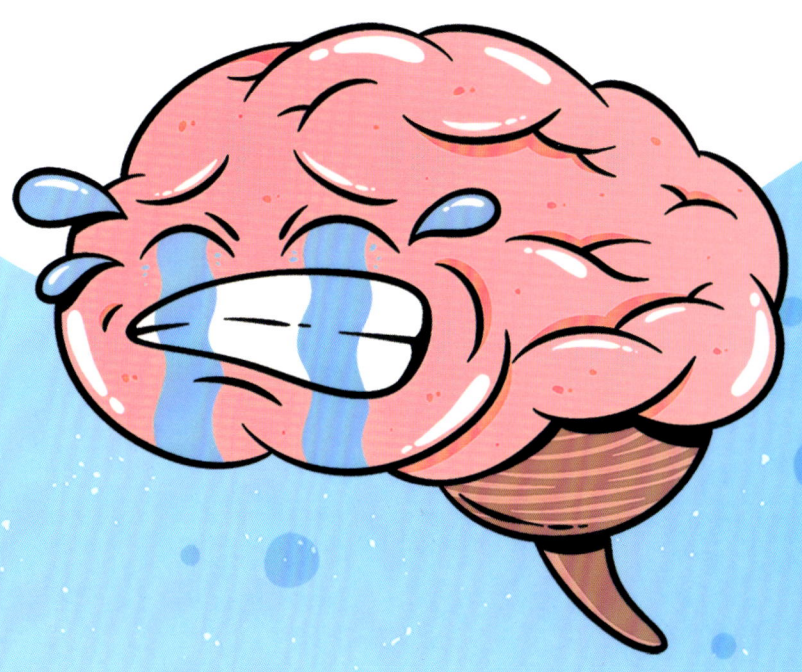

Brain strain

As upside-down time ticks on, the brain starts to swell. Dizziness, blurred vision, and a nasty headache would all develop. Soon, there'd be bleeding inside the brain and blood would pool in the heart. After five to six hours, there'd be a real risk of dying.

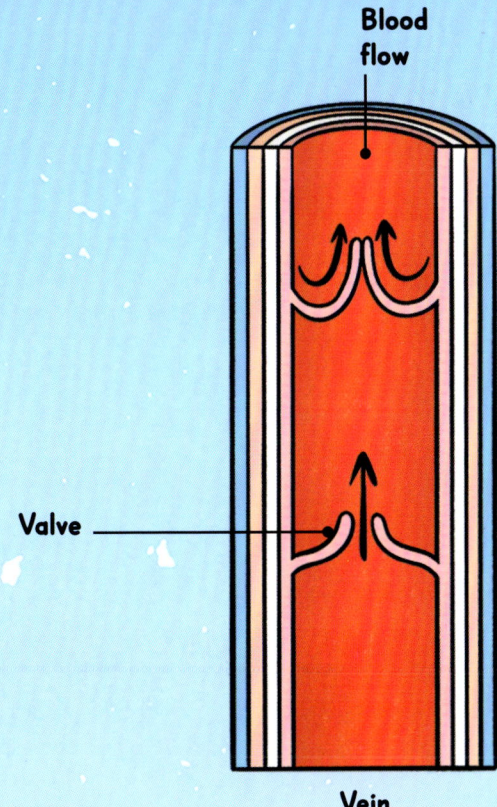

Blood flow

Valve

Vein

Right way up

Your body developed to almost always be the "right" way up (or lying down). Little flaps, called valves, inside your leg veins stop blood from pooling in your feet. And when your leg and feet muscles move, they help to push this blood back towards your heart. Because your brain is above your heart, it doesn't need this system. Gravity does the job. But when you go upside down, there is little to stop blood from pooling in your brain.

Unlike people, bats have vein valves that stop blood pooling in their head.

The answer?

Don't do it! Unless you're in space, that is. There's so little gravity in space that blood wouldn't pool in your head or your heart — so you'd be fine!

What if you could breathe underwater?

Imagine jumping into a swimming pool or the sea and not having to come up for air! All kinds of animals get the oxygen they need while underwater. Great white sharks do it. Even tiny little clownfish do it. So how difficult can it be?

Your very distant ancestors were fish!

Cell energy

Your cells need oxygen to turn the energy in food into a type of fuel that they can use. Unfortunately, in doing this, a TOXIC waste is produced – a gas called carbon dioxide. You, and sharks and clownfish, need a way to get oxygen in and carbon dioxide out.

Gills or lungs?

The job of your lungs is to get oxygen from air into you and carbon dioxide out of you. Fish, including sharks, have gills instead of lungs, which work to do the same job underwater. When water flows over gills, oxygen rushes into the blood inside them and carbon dioxide moves out.

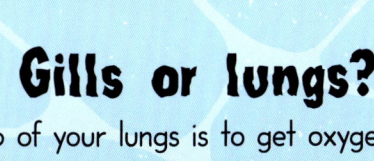

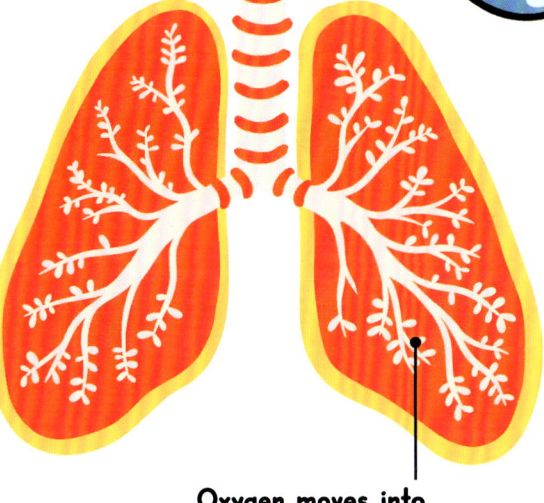

Carbon dioxide moves into your lungs, so you can breathe it out.

Oxygen moves into your blood through the walls of tiny air bags.

Oxygen in, carbon dioxide out

You have two lungs. Both are filled with air tubes. The smallest tubes have bunches of tiny air bags at the end. These air bags are covered in capillaries (the tiniest of the vessels that carry blood). When you breathe in, fresh air enters these air bags. Oxygen then moves through their thin walls into your blood. At the same time, carbon dioxide moves from your blood into the air bags – so you can breathe it out. When you feel like you have to breathe in, that's because there's too much carbon dioxide in your body.

The world record for breath-holding is 24 minutes 37 seconds!

The answer?

Fish gills just can't work in air. Your lungs just can't handle water. While it would be amazing to be able to breathe underwater – you could stare at fish for hours – you won't be able to unless you take a tank of air with you.

Oxygen delivery

All animals need oxygen to survive. Every time you breathe in, fresh oxygen moves from your lungs into your blood. It's immediately snapped up by your red blood cells. Or, to be more precise, by an oxygen-grabbing substance inside these cells called haemoglobin (said hee-moh-GLOH-bin) that then delivers the oxygen to your body's cells.

Each of your red blood cells contains 270 MILLION bits of haemoglobin.

What if your blood turned blue?

Maybe you already know that octopuses have blue blood. They survive just fine. Though they do also have three hearts and a doughnut-shaped brain – but that's another story! Of course, your blood is always red, and there's a good reason for this. But if octopuses can get by with blue blood, could you?

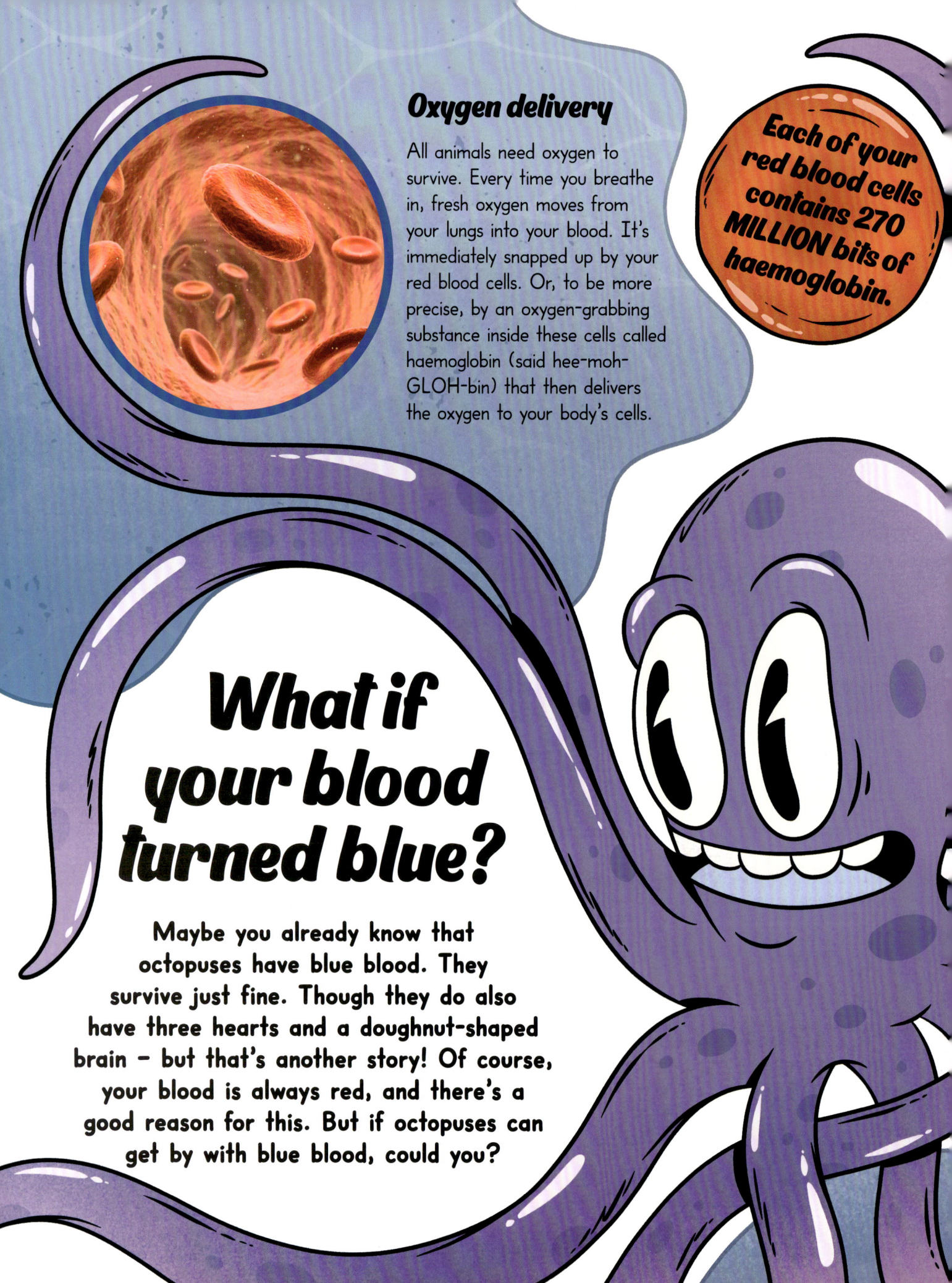

Which metal?

The really vital ingredient in haemoglobin is iron. (Yes, the metal that's sometimes still used for gates and railings). When this iron meets oxygen, and holds onto it, the result is a red colour. Instead of iron, octopuses use another metal, copper. When copper meets oxygen, the result is a blue colour.

Haematite (iron oxide)

Azurite (copper oxide)

Red blood cells with lots of oxygen are bright red.

Octopus blood with lots of oxygen is a vivid blue.

Those with less oxygen are a darker red.

Oxygen

Oxygen

Direction of blood

Red or blue?

Humans get oxygen from air, and it contains plenty. Octopuses, however, live in water, which holds much less oxygen. The octopus's copper-based oxygen-grabber can carry masses more oxygen than ours, though. This is vital for the octopus, but it's not necessary for us. Though your veins can look blue through your skin, your blood is always red. When it's packed with lots of oxygen, it turns bright red. When octopus blood is packed with oxygen, it turns a vivid blue.

Horseshoe crabs and squid have blue blood, too.

The answer?

If your blood's turned blue, you could be turning into an octopus! Too much oxygen is bad for your body, though, so you might have to move into the ocean as well.

25

What if your heart muscle got tired?

You know that the muscles in your arms and legs get tired when you use them a lot. Just think of how you feel after a long day at the park. Your heart is packed with muscle, too, and this muscle works a lot harder than your arms and legs do. But it doesn't ever get tired!

Your heart is about as big as your fist!

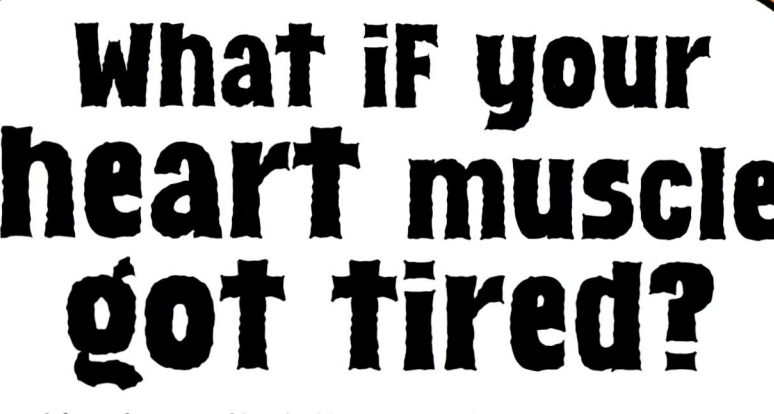

Heart rate

Your heart rate is the number of times your heart muscle tightens, or "beats", to push blood around your body every minute. While you're watching a TV show, it's probably about 70 beats a minute. Unless there are spiders, in which case it might be faster! Either way, your heart never rests, it just speeds up or slows down.

Super muscle

Heart muscle is special. It gets more blood – and so more oxygen – than other muscles. Plus, its cells are PACKED with way more tiny energy generators than other types of muscle. It can also easily switch between using THREE different types of fuel to give it energy. All this means that heart muscle can work and work without getting tired.

Your heart beats more than 100,000 times every day.

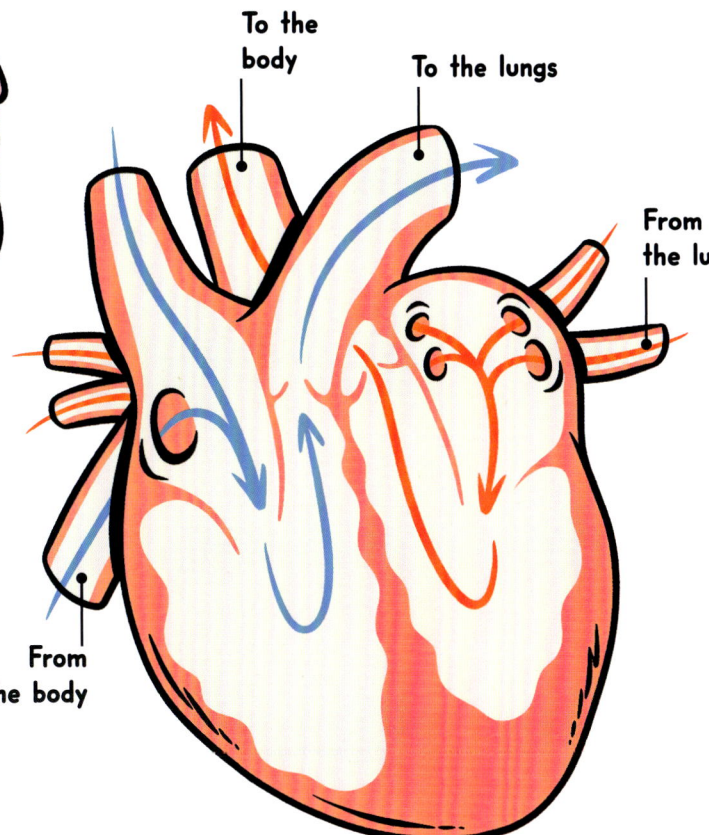

To the body

To the lungs

From the lungs

From the body

Pumping blood

Your heart is a pump. It has one job: to push blood around your body. It pushes "used" blood to your lungs, to pick up oxygen and, at the same time, pushes "fresh" blood out around your body. It does all this automatically. Good thing, too. Just think how often you forget to tidy your bedroom, or brush your hair. Imagine if you had to remember, every second, to think, "Heart – beat!".

"Used" blood coming back from the body is often coloured blue in pictures. However, it's actually red. It's just a darker, duller red than blood that's full of oxygen.

The answer?

Your heart's job is to pump blood around your body, to keep your cells alive and working properly. So it's a good thing that your heart muscle doesn't get tired. If it did, you'd become very unwell.

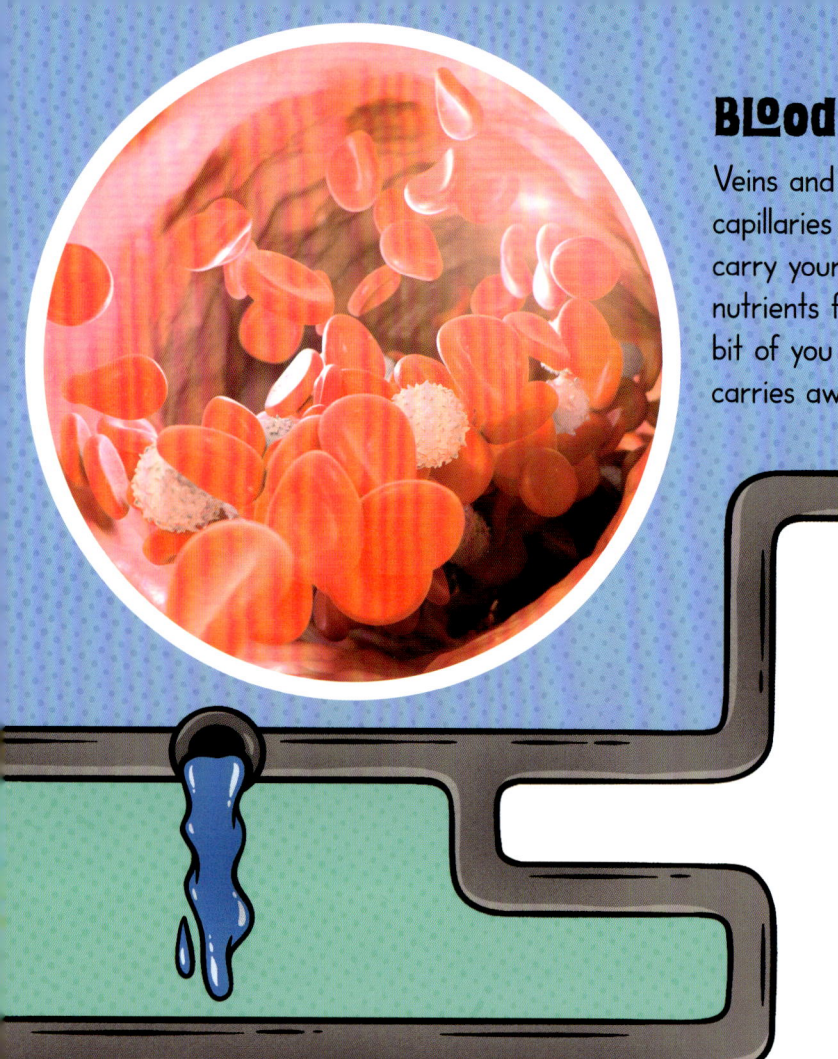

Blood network

Veins and arteries are like main roads, while your capillaries are like lanes that come off them. They carry your blood, which contains good stuff, such as nutrients from food and oxygen, into almost every bit of you – including your eyeballs. Blood also carries away dangerous waste, like carbon dioxide.

What if your veins were made of metal?

Your veins are tubes that carry precious blood, and so are your arteries and capillaries. Of course, if you lose your blood, you will die, so why are these vital tubes made of delicate, easily cuttable stuff? What if they were made of strong steel instead?

By adulthood, you'll have 100,000 KM (60,000 MILES) of blood vessels inside your body. That's enough to reach more than twice around the world.

28

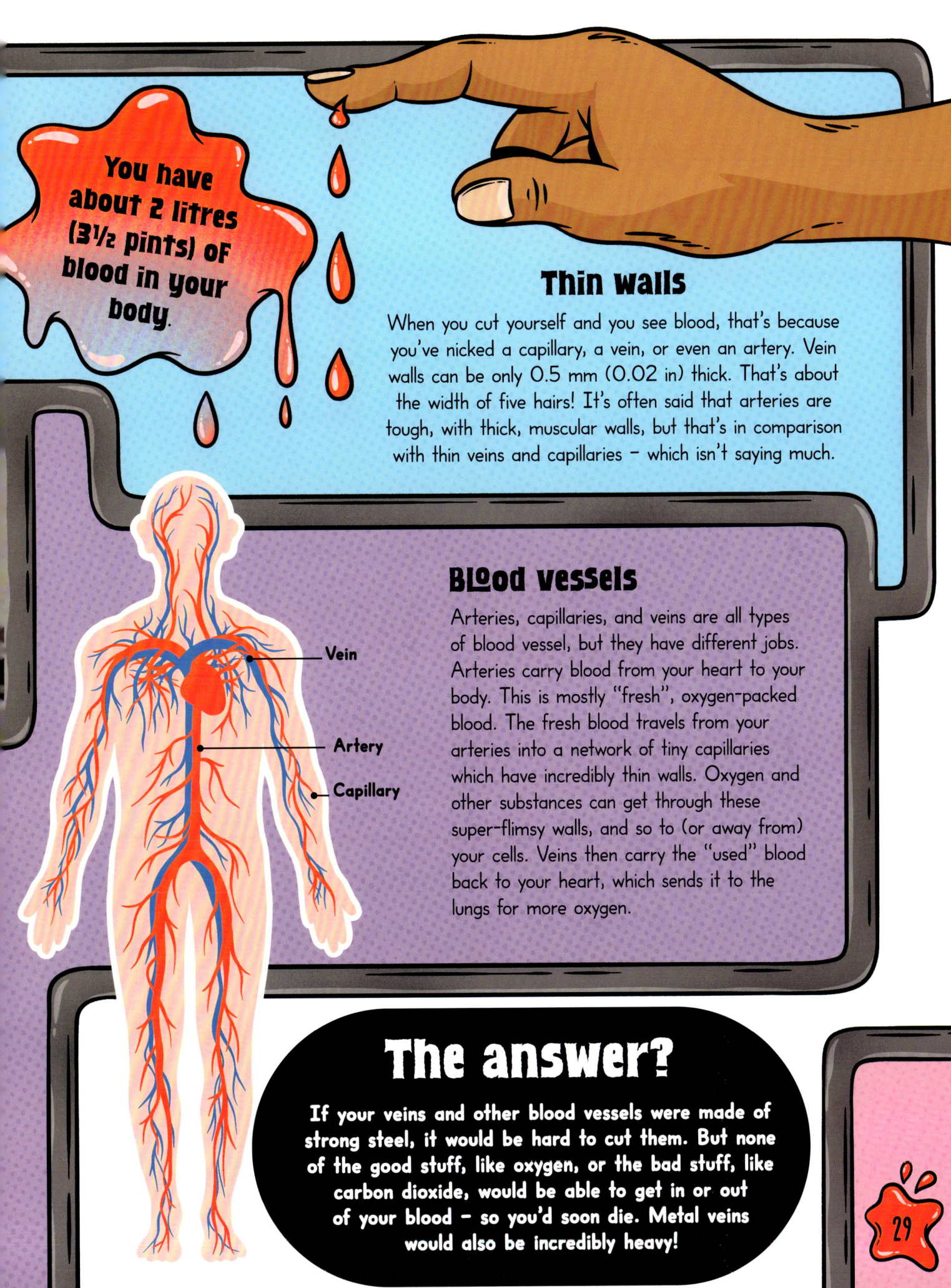

You have about 2 litres (3½ pints) of blood in your body.

Thin walls

When you cut yourself and you see blood, that's because you've nicked a capillary, a vein, or even an artery. Vein walls can be only 0.5 mm (0.02 in) thick. That's about the width of five hairs! It's often said that arteries are tough, with thick, muscular walls, but that's in comparison with thin veins and capillaries – which isn't saying much.

Vein

Artery

Capillary

Blood vessels

Arteries, capillaries, and veins are all types of blood vessel, but they have different jobs. Arteries carry blood from your heart to your body. This is mostly "fresh", oxygen-packed blood. The fresh blood travels from your arteries into a network of tiny capillaries which have incredibly thin walls. Oxygen and other substances can get through these super-flimsy walls, and so to (or away from) your cells. Veins then carry the "used" blood back to your heart, which sends it to the lungs for more oxygen.

The answer?

If your veins and other blood vessels were made of strong steel, it would be hard to cut them. But none of the good stuff, like oxygen, or the bad stuff, like carbon dioxide, would be able to get in or out of your blood – so you'd soon die. Metal veins would also be incredibly heavy!

29

What if your liver and nose swapped places?

Your liver sits deep inside you, just above your stomach – and your nose? Well, your nose developed to work in air, not your insides. So, you wouldn't be able to smell cake, or farts, or anything. But what else would change?

Sweet spot

Your liver is your body's sweet shop. It holds stocks of sugar, all stored away for when you need them. When the amount of sugar in your blood (your blood sugar level) gets a bit low – a few hours after your last meal, maybe, or after you've been running around – your liver chucks some more sugar in.

Your liver is mostly on your right side.

Many jobs

Making bile is one of your liver's crucial jobs. After getting squeezed into the small intestine, bile acts like a chemical ninja on fats in food: it attacks them, and smashes them up. This is an important part of the process of getting fatty fragments into your blood so they can be used by the body. Your liver also cleans your blood and it puts some of the waste and toxins it collects into bile, sending them on a journey to one smelly exit, in poo.

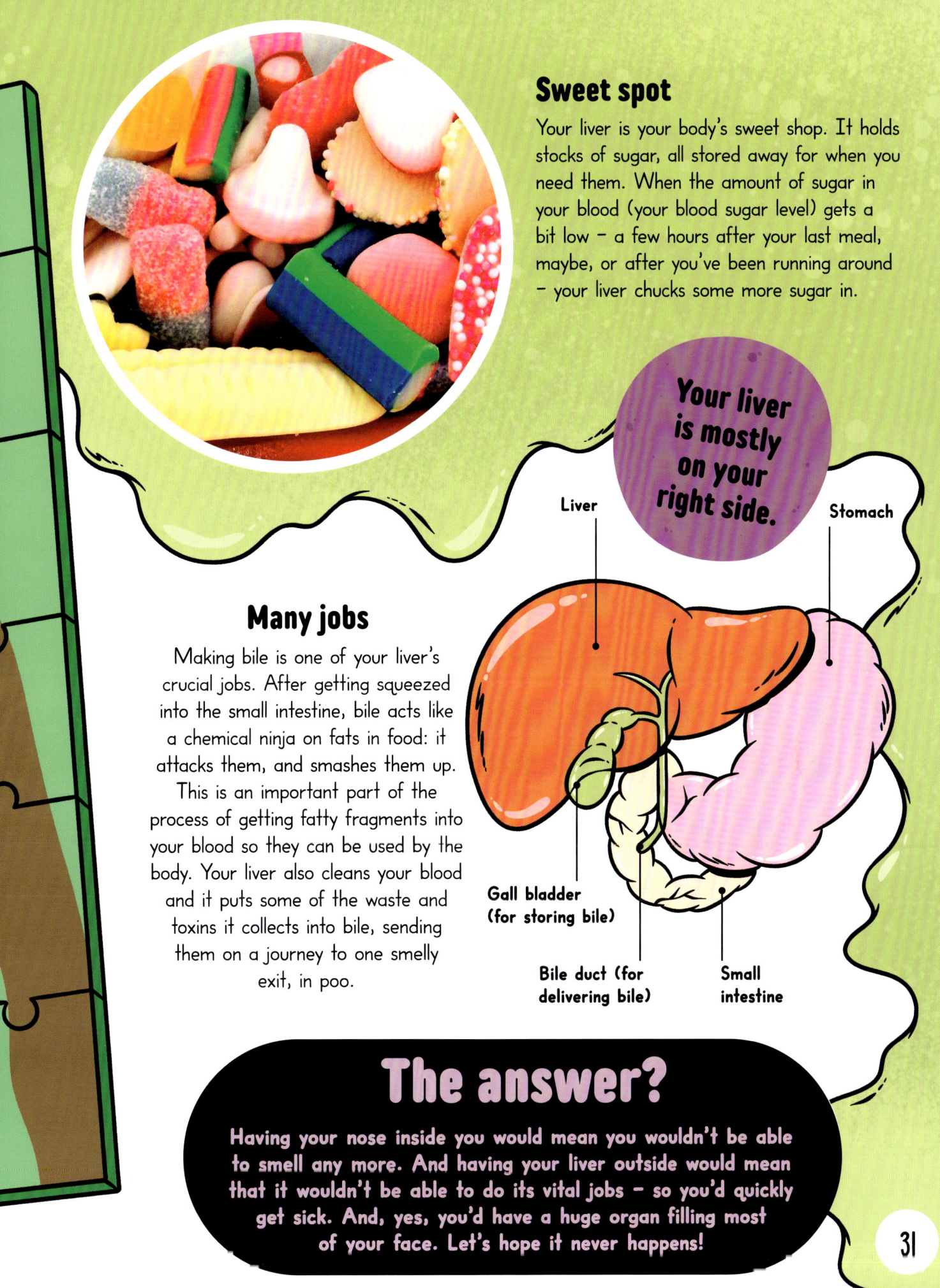

Liver

Stomach

Gall bladder
(for storing bile)

Bile duct (for
delivering bile)

Small
intestine

The answer?

Having your nose inside you would mean you wouldn't be able to smell any more. And having your liver outside would mean that it wouldn't be able to do its vital jobs – so you'd quickly get sick. And, yes, you'd have a huge organ filling most of your face. Let's hope it never happens!

Tough plants

Your stomach is a bit like a drive-in car wash. Only instead of rollers, it has rippling muscles. And rather than water, it blasts out acid. This treatment reduces most food to mush. But grass cells have very thick, sturdy walls that are hard to break down. (Cotton fibre cells have even sturdier walls. That's why you can't eat your T-shirt for lunch.)

Cow stomachs contain bacteria that SMASH grass into sugar.

What if you ate a BOWL OF GRASS?

Grass is tough, and the "blades" have sharp edges. So chewing on some would do your teeth and mouth no good. Also, some grasses are TOXIC. Even non-toxic grass could make you throw up if you ate it. But if you did manage to keep some down, then what?

Small intestine

After your stomach, the bits of grass would move into your small intestine. This is where most of the good things in food — the nutrients — are broken down into bits that are small enough to get into your blood. This process is called digestion. Grass cell walls are packed with energy stores, but your small intestine doesn't have the tools to get at them.

Large intestine

After the small intestine, the mushed up grass would travel into your large intestine (a perfect, if boring, name). Here, "friendly" bacteria help to get the last scraps of nutrients out of your food. But the types of bacteria that can tackle grass cells don't live inside humans — so you still wouldn't be able to break them down. In the large intestine, extra water is taken out of the food slurry, too. The result is... poo. The poo of a kid who ate grass would be full of bits of slightly soggy-looking grass!

Food travels down here

Stomach

Large intestine

Small intestine

Poo store (rectum)

Your LARGE INTESTINE is nearly as long as you are — ABOUT 1 M (3 FT)!

The answer?

Even if you can keep it down, grass is not worth eating. And it would be very hard on your poor teeth. Don't do it!

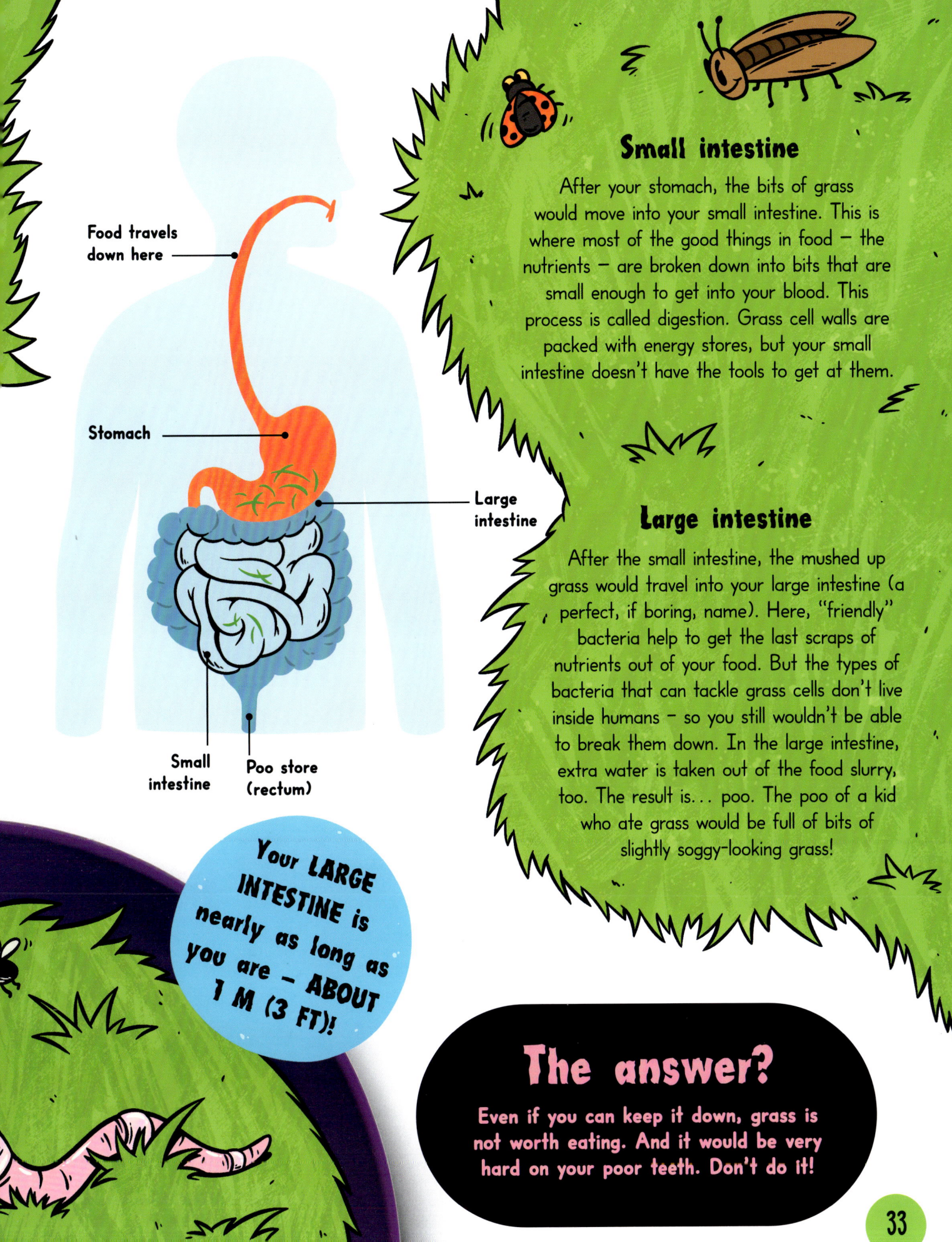

33

What if you never **threw** **up** again?

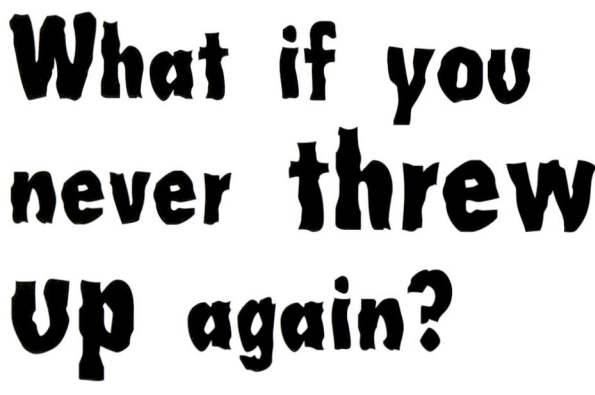

When you vomit, the contents of your stomach come back up out of your mouth. Sometimes also your nose. No one likes it. It's horrible and smelly, and it can make your tummy hurt and your throat burn. If it never happened again, you'd be happy... right?

ORANGE VOMIT IS PARTIALLY DIGESTED FOOD.

THE PUKE LIST
All these things can make your brain issue the command: "Throw up!":

- Rotten food
- Germ-laden drinks
- Infections
- Poisons

Ideally, you'll eject anything bad before it can damage your body. So, even the smell of sick can make you throw up. Why? Because if someone around you is being sick, your brain assumes it's down to something they ate and that you probably ate the same stuff — so you'd better puke, too!

Travel sick

Travel sickness is so unfair. It's thought to happen because a swaying motion can create some of the same sensations as a poison. Of course, if you have swallowed poison, it's a good idea to get rid of it. So you vomit.

To mouth

Diaphragm

Stomach

Stomach squeeze

Right before you throw up, your mouth fills with extra spit, to protect it from the stomach acid that's about to come in. Then, the layer of muscle under your lungs, called the diaphragm (said DAI-a-fram) pushes on your stomach. Your airway shuts, to stop you breathing in sick. And muscles in your tummy region start their own stomach squeeze. The result... what was down comes back up!

The answer?

While a swaying motion is not a good reason for throwing up, most are excellent. If you didn't ever vomit, you'd get more sick more often. And if you didn't get rid of dangerous germs or poisons, you could even die!

What if you stored all your POOS in a pile?

That would be a seriously stinky pile! But how big would it be? The bigger you are – and the bigger you get as you grow – the bigger and heavier your poos become. So, if we consider all your poos from birth to the age of 10, say, what would that look like?

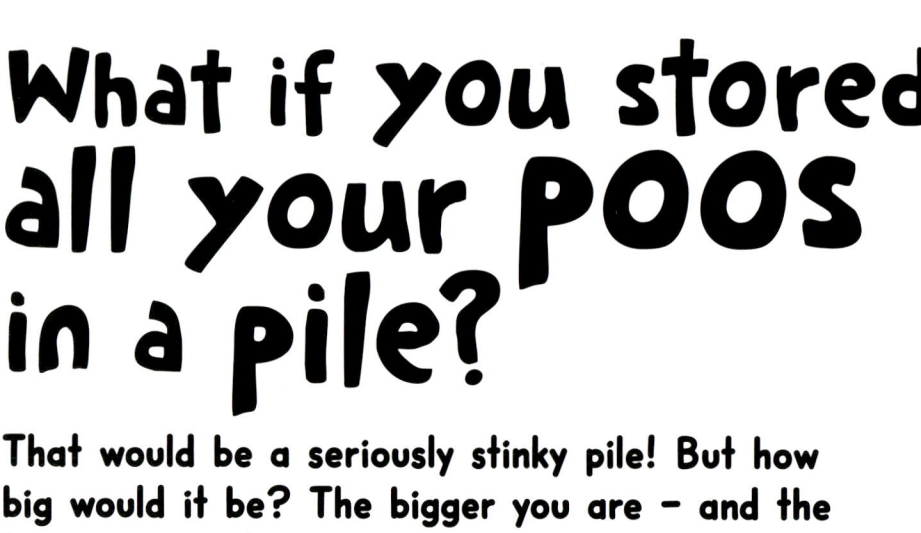

An adult's yearly poos weigh about the same as a pig.

Daily poo

What you eat can have a big impact on how much poo your body makes. This means there's a huge range in how much it's "normal" to poo. An average 8 year old might push out about 150 g (5 oz) every day. That's roughly the weight of a baseball, but that poo would take up a bit more space than a baseball.

Sugary foods make for stinkier poo.

Running around helps to move poo through your body.

Sweetcorn test

It takes around 24–36 hours for food to turn from a tasty mouthful... to poo. You can test this yourself. Eat some sweetcorn and note down the day and the time. Then, keep an eye on your poos. You're watching for the presence of the tough outer yellow husks.

Type 1:
Hard, lumpy poo suggests bad constipation.

Type 2:
Also suggests you're not pooing often enough.

Type 3:
A hard, cracked sausage isn't ideal, either.

Type 4:
A soft, smooth sausage is what you're after!

Type 5:
Soft blobs suggest you've eaten more fibre than usual.

Type 6:
Mushy poo is OK, if you're well and there's a reason for it (like extra fibre).

Type 7:
Liquid poo, called diarrhoea, could mean you have a tummy bug.

The poo chart

Poo is what's left when your body has got all the nutrients it can from your food – and chucked in some extra waste. It contains: bits of food you can't digest, like sweetcorn husks; bacteria from your gut; water; and a brown chemical made after old red blood cells have been broken down.

It's this that gives poo its colour. Poo comes in many different shapes depending on what you've eaten or if you are ill. The poo chart helps you understand what your poo can tell you about your body.

The answer?

There's such a huge range in what's normal (and healthy) that your lifetime poo pile could easily be far bigger – or smaller – than your best friend's. But, by the age of 10, an average kid might have produced about 415 kg (915 lb) of poo. That's about the weight of a horse!

Doctors call farts "flatus".

What if you couldn't fart?

Are farts: a) funny or b) mostly gas produced by bacteria as they feast on bits of leftover food in your gut? The answer is: definitely "b" and sometimes "a"! If you couldn't fart this gut gas out, the world would be a sweeter-smelling place. But some pretty shocking things would happen, too...

Mouth farts

If you couldn't fart, some of the fart gas would get absorbed into your blood. It would then go to your lungs, for you to breathe out. This would make your breath smell bad.

Burst intestine

Your large intestine, where the fart-producing bacteria live, would begin to inflate like a balloon. This would hurt. In weeks (rather than days or months), your large intestine would burst. Unlike a balloon, it wouldn't burst with a bang, but holes would appear in it and its contents would spill into your body – which can be fatal!

BANG!

Gut gas

Gas made by hungry gut bacteria normally passes into your rectum – or your poo store – and then out of your anus. Certain foods are more likely than others to lead to lots of stinky farts. Beans, lentils, sugary foods, onions, and fatty foods are all on this list. Burps are a bit different to farts. They're mostly gas that you have swallowed, but that hasn't got all the way from your mouth to your stomach, so it comes back up. Fizzy drinks can cause burps, as can gobbling your food too fast.

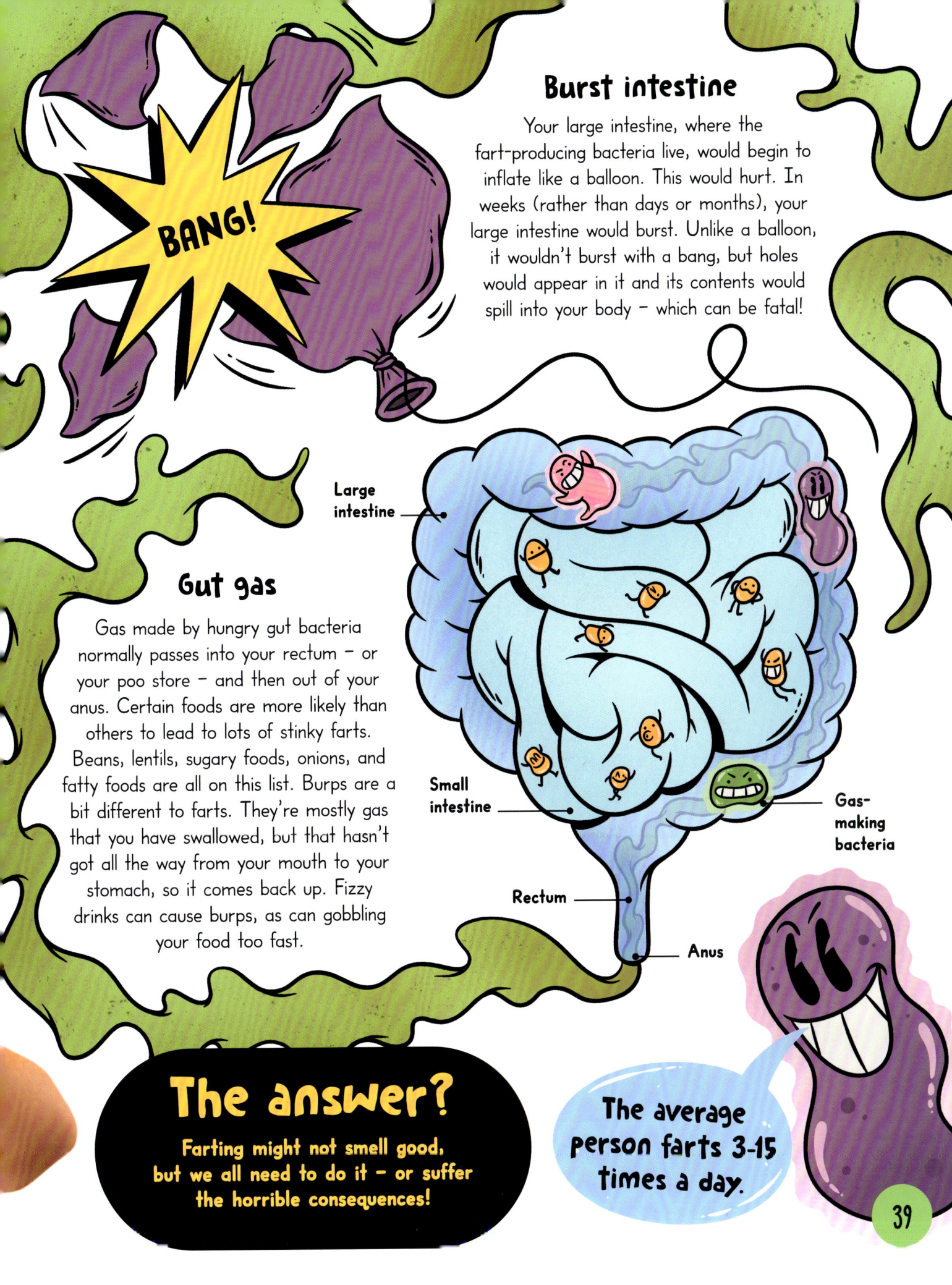

Large intestine

Small intestine

Rectum

Anus

Gas-making bacteria

The answer?

Farting might not smell good, but we all need to do it – or suffer the horrible consequences!

The average person farts 3-15 times a day.

39

What if you only ate cockroaches for a year?

Cockroaches might not be on the menu where you live. But in some countries, people farm and eat them. In fact, insects are considered perfect munching material in lots of parts of the world. If you ate cockroaches, and nothing else, though, what would happen to you?

Nutritious snack

Many insects are great sources of protein, which help muscle, skin, and other bits of you grow. They also contain fats, which give you energy, and some important minerals, including: calcium (which is essential for strong teeth and bones), iron (for red blood cells and muscles), and zinc (which you need to grow).

Some insects must have their outer skeleton removed before being eaten – it's a choking hazard!

Some types of insect are poisonous to eat – never eat an insect from the wild!

Edible insects

Fancy a lunch of fried locusts, mealworms, or crickets? These popular edible insects are seen as alternatives to meats like chicken, pork, and beef, although some people are allergic to insects. They're also cheap and very easy to farm. No fields required! Only farmed insects are safe to eat, though, and they must be cooked to kill any bad bacteria inside them.

Edible insects are often deep-fried!

Other

Fat

Protein

Twenty a day

A kid would have to eat only about 20 Madagascar hissing cockroaches a day to get enough energy, and more than enough protein. However, cockroaches don't contain all the vitamins your body needs to be healthy. Without vitamin C, you'd develop weak bone, lose teeth, and have bleeding gums.

The answer?

After a year, your body would be suffering from a lack of some vital vitamins. But you'd probably still be alive. And desperate to eat anything but a cockroach!

41

LOTS OF WATER!

You are seriously watery. In fact, just OVER HALF of your body weight is WATER! Among other things, it:

- Makes your blood runny
- Keeps your cells in shape
- Lets you get rid of waste, in wee
- Allows you to sweat, to cool down
- Forms saliva in your mouth – and snot in your nose!

After lots of exercise, milk is better than a sports drink to top up your water levels.

What if you were allergic

Some people are allergic to water. Rain or a bath can bring their skin out in an itchy rash – so they have to take a lot of care when washing. This doesn't happen to their throat or stomach when they drink water, though. Which is a very good thing, as you'll see.

Juicy fruits, like oranges, are great food sources of water.

Stay hydrated

You know that feeling when you just have to run to the tap? That happens when the water monitoring bit of your brain triggers the "THIRST" alarm. When you've had a good drink, it cancels the alarm. You shouldn't wait until you're desperate, though. It's important for your health — and your performance in lessons — to drink water regularly.

TEARS

BREATH

SWEAT

POO

WEE

Water loss

You lose water through your mouth when you breathe, through your skin when you sweat, in tears, and in your wee and poo. Kids are often told to make sure to drink 6-8 glasses of fluid every day to keep their water levels up. But if you've been running around or it's hot, and you've been sweating a lot, you'll need more water than you do on lazier or cooler days. It's important to replace the water you've lost to keep your body healthy.

to water?

The answer?

Your body is chock-full of water. It's absolutely vital for life. For people with a skin allergy to water, daily life can be tricky. If you were allergic to the water that you drank, though, you would die.

What if you took a bath in wee?

It sounds disgusting! But the ancient Romans used human wee to clean their clothes. As did people living in England in the time of Queen Victoria. So, should you think about weeing into the bath, instead of turning on the tap?

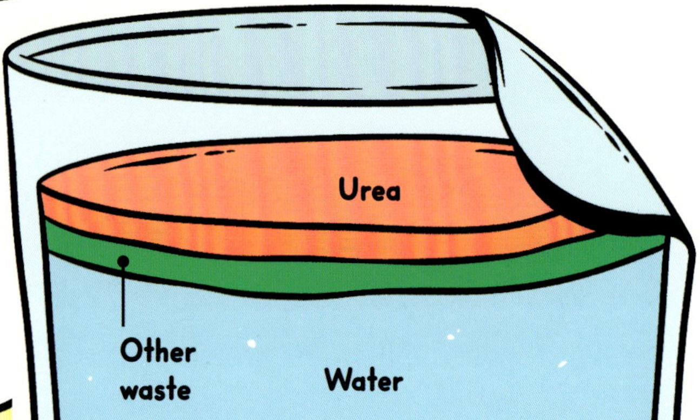

Urea

Other waste

Water

What is wee?

Wee is 95 per cent water. Another 2.5 per cent is "urea" (said yoo-REE-a), a waste substance made when your body breaks down proteins from food. The rest is made up of some other things that your body wants to get rid of, including an acid called uric acid and excess sugar.

Eating lots of carrots can give your wee an orange tint.

Whiffy wee

When wee is left to sit, bacteria will feast on the urea that's in it and create a stinky chemical called ammonia (said a-MOH-nee-a). Ammonia breaks down fat. This is why stale wee was once used to get rid of fatty, greasy stains on clothes. BUT the ammonia and uric acid in wee will irritate skin, and could make it sting.

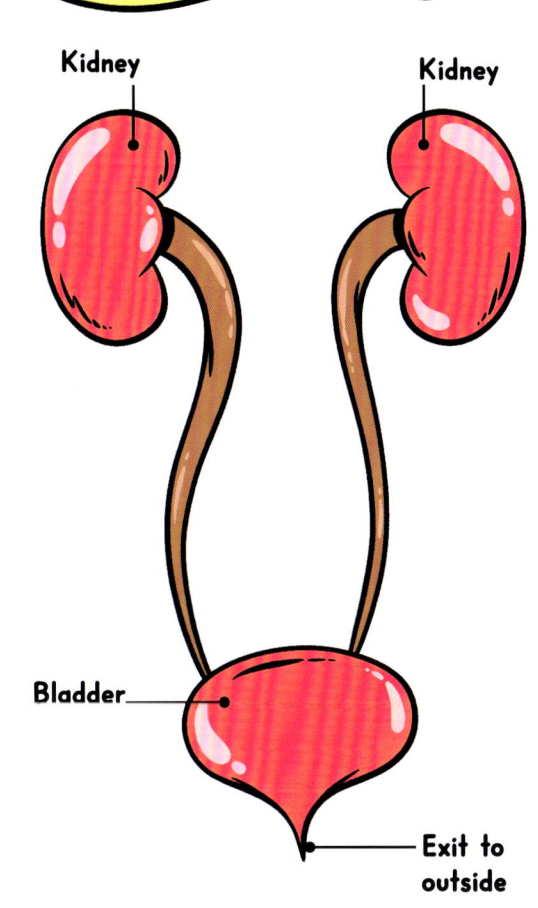

Kidney

Kidney

Bladder

Exit to outside

Making wee

Your kidneys filter your blood, to create wee, or "urine". This urine travels through tubes to your bladder. When your bladder fills, it swells like a balloon. Stretch sensors in the wall of your bladder register this, and send signals to your brain — and you feel the need to wee. Kids should produce about 1 litre (2 pints) of urine every day — that's about three soda cans' worth. If you're drinking enough water, it will be light yellow.

The answer?

A quick bath in wee wouldn't hurt you, but it wouldn't be good for your skin, either. If you were to sit in a wee bath for hours, though, it would make your skin red and sore. Don't do it!

It would take you about six months to fill a bath with wee.

45

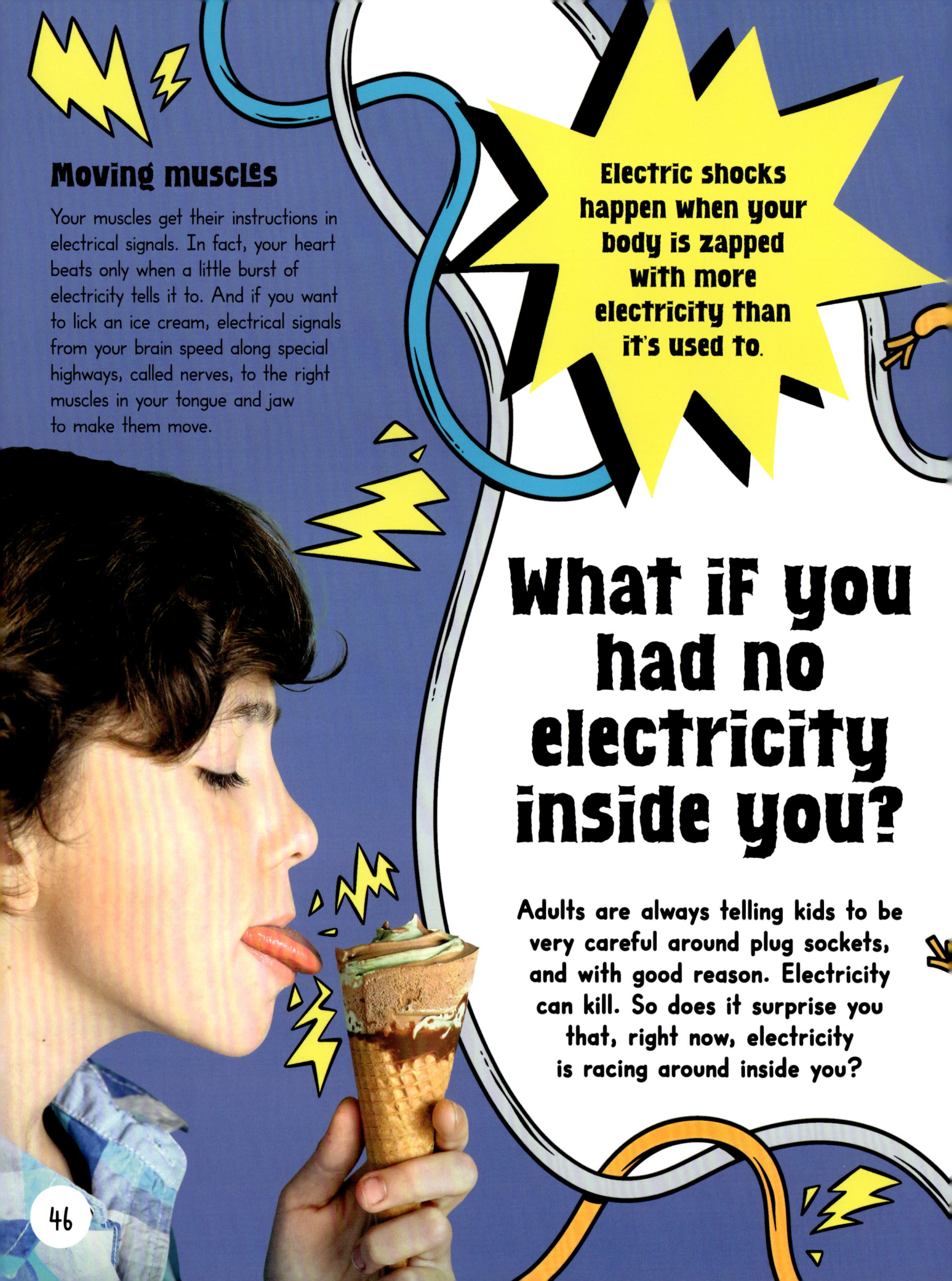

Moving muscles

Your muscles get their instructions in electrical signals. In fact, your heart beats only when a little burst of electricity tells it to. And if you want to lick an ice cream, electrical signals from your brain speed along special highways, called nerves, to the right muscles in your tongue and jaw to make them move.

Electric shocks happen when your body is zapped with more electricity than it's used to.

What if you had no electricity inside you?

Adults are always telling kids to be very careful around plug sockets, and with good reason. Electricity can kill. So does it surprise you that, right now, electricity is racing around inside you?

BRAIN POWER

Without electricity, your brain would be a wobbly, useless blob. That's because it's packed with cells called neurons that use electrical signals to communicate. It's not just neurons that make electricity, though. The thin wall, or "membrane", of each of your cells also acts like a tiny battery.

Electrical signals race around your body at up to 435 kph (270 mph).

Brain

Spinal cord

Nerves

Body wires

Neurons aren't just found in your brain. These tree-shaped cells have long, thin "trunks". Nerves are bundles of these trunks that run around your body like wires. Their job is to carry electrical signals between your brain and spinal cord and other body parts, including your stomach, your lungs, your hands, your tongue, your nose, and your eyes. Without these nerves, your brain and body couldn't communicate, so you wouldn't have any senses and your muscles would be limp.

The answer?

If there was no electricity inside you, you couldn't lick an ice cream, or read this page. Or run. Or smell. Or breathe. Oh, and your heart wouldn't beat. Yes... you'd be dead!

What if you could turn INVISIBLE?

Wouldn't that be amazing? Just think of all the things you could do, and no one would know – or no one would know it was you! No end of stories feature clothes or jewellery that make the wearer invisible. So, could this happen in real life?

An eyeball weighs about the same as a pencil. Inside it is filled with a clear, jelly-like goop.

Dark spots

Your eyes evolved to work well during the day. But for about 10 per cent of your waking hours, you see nothing. This is when you blink – which you do more than 900 times every hour! Your brain fills in these gaps in seeing, so you don't usually notice them.

You blink more than 12,500 times every day!

Invisibility cloak

Scientists are working on ways to make people invisible. One idea is to use a fabric that soaks up light. If you covered yourself in a cloak of this fabric, it would stop light bouncing off you – and so stop other people from seeing you.

The retina detects light

Light enters your eye through a hole (your pupil)

Electrical signals go to the brain

I see you!

For someone to see you, light has to bounce off you and enter their eyes. At the back of each eye is a curved light receiver, called the retina. Some cells in the retina react to the slightest bit of light, but don't let us see in colour. These are called "rods". Others, called "cones", only work well when there's plenty of light. But they allow us to see about a MILLION different colours!

The answer?

Right now, there are only two ways for you to turn invisible: make sure there's NO light around – or get everyone else to shut their eyes!

49

What if you could hear like a bat?

What's the highest sound you can think of? A wailing siren? A chirping bird? Your teacher's shriek when you explain what would happen if you took off all your skin? Bats – and dogs and cats – can hear sounds even higher than that. If you could, too, what would life be like?

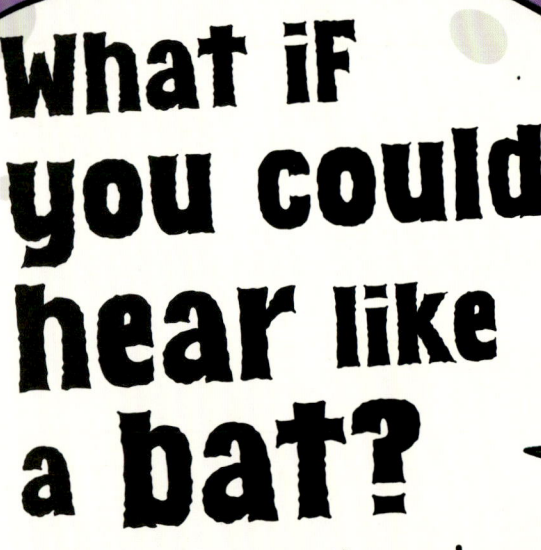

A type of frog that lives in Brazil screams in ultrasound to scare off predators!

Pet sounds

The sounds that humans can hear are called, wait for it... "sound". Sound that is too low for us to hear is called "infrasound". Sound that is too high is called "ultrasound". Dogs and cats can hear some ultrasound, but bats can hear really high ultrasound, beyond the hope of any pet.

Bat chat

Many bats communicate using ultrasound. Some other animals do, too. Baby mice, for example. Dogs and cats can hear these calls because their ancestors evolved to chase and eat rodents. Bats that use ultrasound also use it to get around at night. They make a call, and listen to the echoes that bounce back off the objects around them.

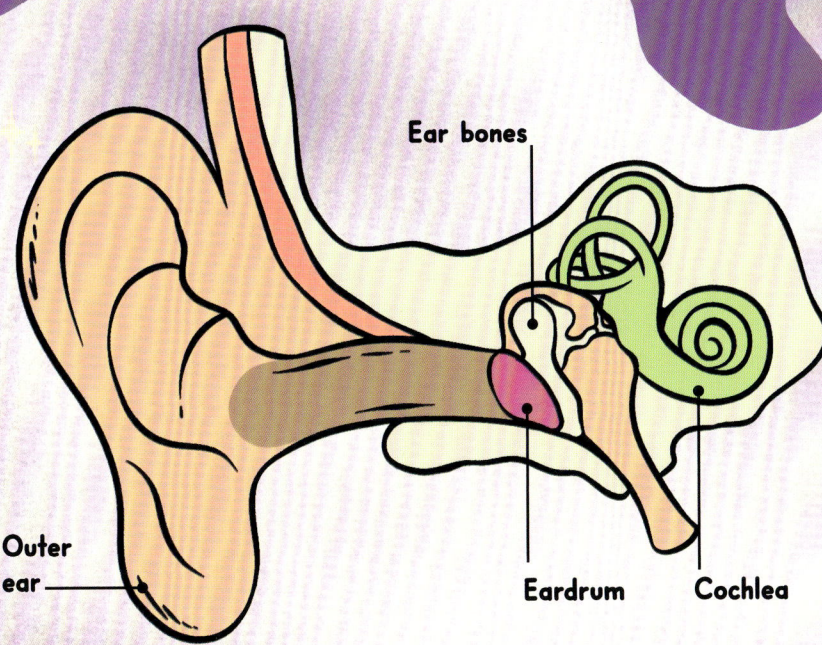

Ear bones

Outer ear

Eardrum

Cochlea

Hairy ears

When sound waves enter your ear, they hit your eardrum, which makes three tiny bones vibrate. These vibrations then pass into a spiral-shaped tube, called the cochlea (said KOK-lee-a). Inside the cochlea are hairy hearing cells. When the hairs get bent by the vibrations, the cells send signals to your brain — and you hear something. Low sounds mostly bend hairs in the upper part. High sounds mostly bend hairs in the lower part. In bats that use ultrasound, the hairy section in the lower part of their cochlea is especially sensitive.

Loud screams - or even singing - can shatter glass!

The answer?

The world would sound very different! You'd be able to hear super-high calls, not just from bats, but baby mice, as well as dolphins and certain whales — not to mention worried frogs!

We like the taste of a bit of salt because our bodies need some salt, but not too much.

Have you ever bitten into a slice of lemon? Lemons are super sour!

Yuck or yum?

Taste tells you what's good to swallow — and what you should spit out. We evolved to taste sugar because it's a source of quick, easy energy. This makes it a good thing, in theory. A bitter taste, though, can mean POISON. Confusingly, some foods, such as broccoli, can also taste bitter, but they are good for you!

What if you couldn't taste sugar?

Imagine biting into a juicy strawberry or a slice of a cake, and it not being sweet. That's what would happen if you couldn't taste sugar. But why do we taste it, why do so many of us love the taste, and what else might happen if foods didn't taste sweet any more?

Sweet overload

Humans really like the taste of sugar. When our distant ancestors came across a sugar-packed food – most often fruit – it was good for them to gobble up that energy. However, they didn't have sweet shops or supermarkets. Most of us now eat too much sugar because a) we love the taste and b) it's in LOTS of foods that are easily available.

SOUR

BITTER

SWEET

Five tastes

There are five basic tastes. Sweet (from sugars), sour (from vitamin C in fruit, for example, or yogurts), bitter (broccoli and cabbage taste bitter to most people), salty (from salt!), and umami (which is the savoury taste of meat, tomatoes, and mushrooms). Now, stick your tongue out – in front of a mirror, not your teacher! Can you see lots of tiny bumps? They contain "taste buds", which are little clusters of taste cells. Each taste cell responds to one of the five basic tastes, such as sweet. Taste cells are also dotted around the inside of your mouth, and the back of your throat.

SALTY

UMAMI

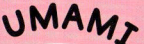

The answer?

Sugary foods and drinks wouldn't taste sweet any more, so wouldn't be as yummy. But this might stop you eating too much sugar!

Sniff school

Scientists in America drizzled a chocolate-scented liquid in a zig-zagging line across a field. Then they asked blindfolded volunteers to go down on their hands and knees and try to smell their way along this trail. Most could do it, or soon learned to do it!

Humans can smell about a **TRILLION DIFFERENT** smells.

What if you had a dog's nose?

Dogs are famous super-sniffers. They can identify another dog just from the whiff of its old wee. And they can track scent trails left by people for miles. But if you were to go about on all fours, nose to the ground, you might be surprised by what you could do...

Stink stops

The more you use your sense of smell, the better it will get. Try to stop and smell as many different objects as you can when you're walking around at home. Including the stinky ones! How many can you count?

A STUDY OF PEOPLE FROM AROUND THE WORLD FOUND THAT VANILLA AND PEACHES ARE OUR FAVOURITE SMELLS – AND SWEATY FEET ARE THE WORST!

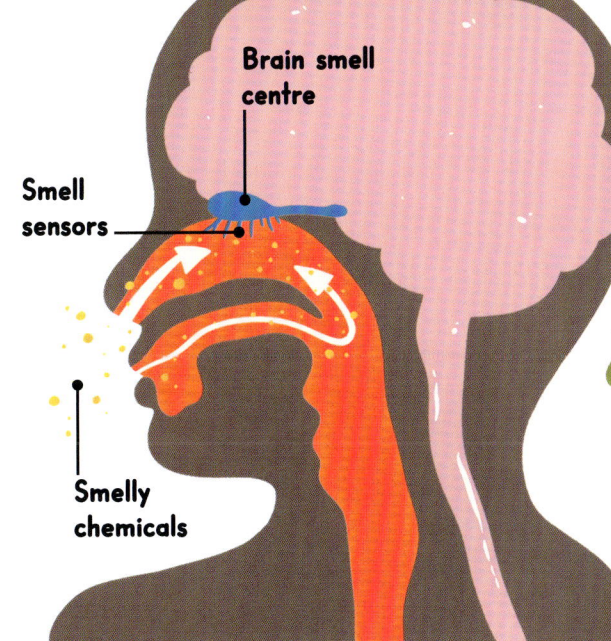

Brain smell centre

Smell sensors

Smelly chemicals

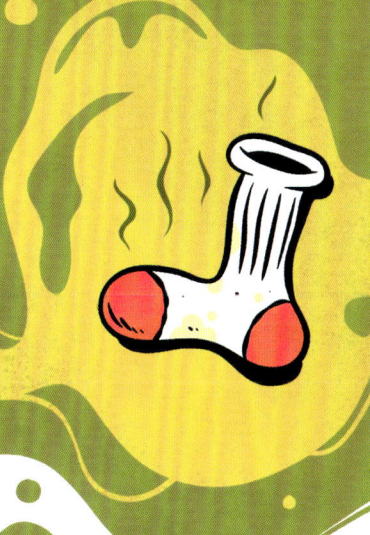

Nose to brain

For you to smell something, chemicals have to travel in the air to sensors high up in your nose. You have about 400 different types of smell sensor. Based on the pattern of signals that they send to your brain, you know whether you're smelling a ripe peach – or sweaty feet!

The answer?

Your human nose is actually pretty good. And it might feel strange to have a dog's wet nose!

Early sense

At its most basic, touch tells you where your body ends and the rest of the world begins. This form of touch developed in some of Earth's earliest life forms. Today, every living thing – including bacteria and moss – can sense when it's in contact with something else.

What if you couldn't touch your toes?

Not because your body isn't bendy enough. But, what if you reached down and your fingertips connected with your toes – but you felt nothing? Or you took a step – but your foot couldn't feel the ground? We take touch for granted. But what would life be like without it?

Fantastic fingers

You feel using touch sensors in your skin. The skin on your chest and back has 100 times fewer of these sensors in every square centimetre than the skin on your fingertips. Try brushing the tip of a pencil across a fingertip and then your back. You'll feel the difference!

Not very sensitive ← → Very sensitive

Touch trio

Touch is really a group of three senses. Pressure touch tells you when something is in contact with you. That might be your own fingertips, your clothes, or a spider! Vibration touch tells you, with your eyes shut, whether you're running your fingertips across glass, silk, wood, or even a worm. Emotional touch is the slow-moving, warm touch of another person. This type of touch tells a newborn baby that it's safe. But as we grow up, most of us still crave it.

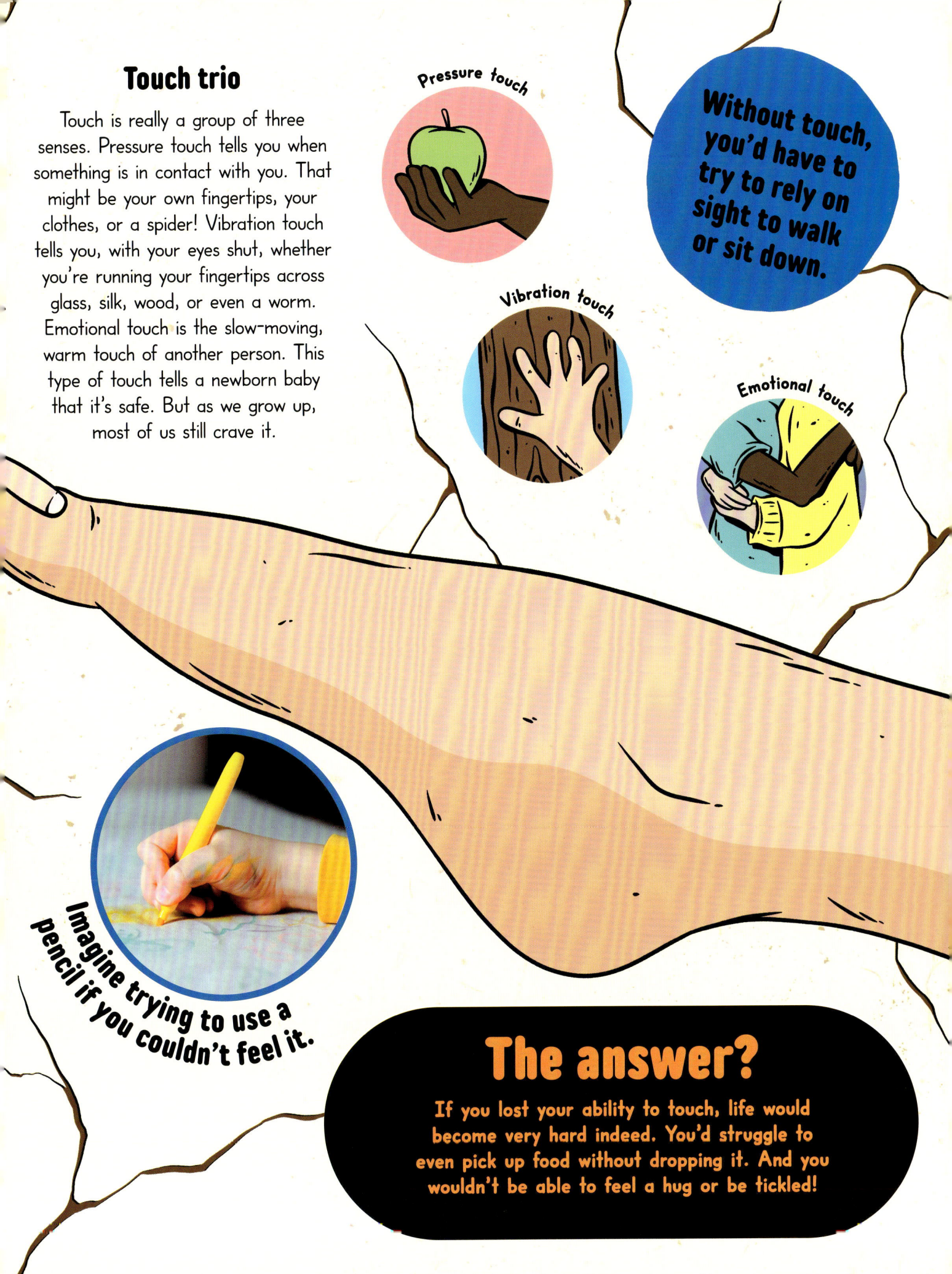

Pressure touch

Vibration touch

Emotional touch

Without touch, you'd have to try to rely on sight to walk or sit down.

Imagine trying to use a pencil if you couldn't feel it.

The answer?

If you lost your ability to touch, life would become very hard indeed. You'd struggle to even pick up food without dropping it. And you wouldn't be able to feel a hug or be tickled!

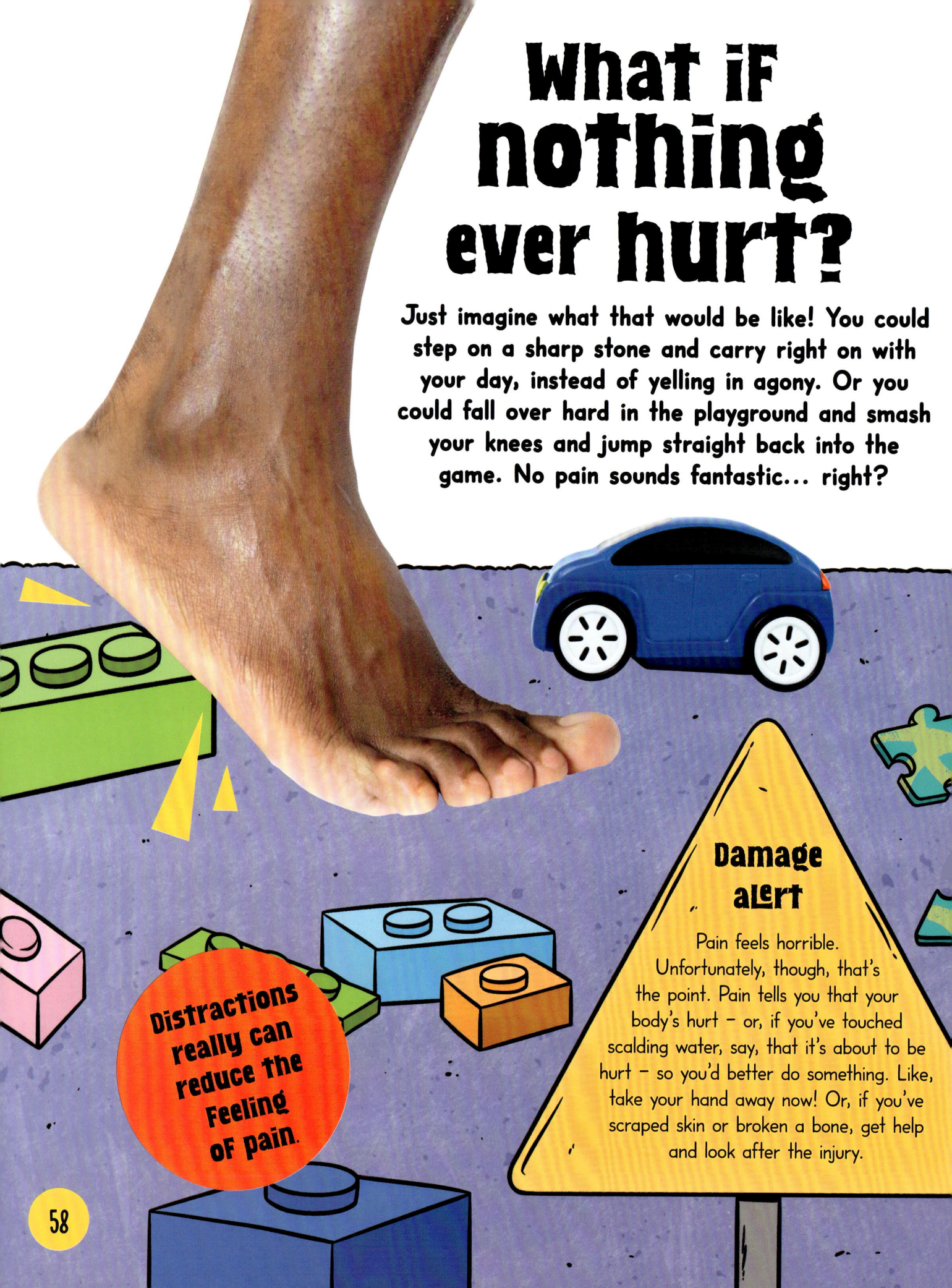

What if nothing ever hurt?

Just imagine what that would be like! You could step on a sharp stone and carry right on with your day, instead of yelling in agony. Or you could fall over hard in the playground and smash your knees and jump straight back into the game. No pain sounds fantastic... right?

Distractions really can reduce the feeling of pain.

Damage alert

Pain feels horrible. Unfortunately, though, that's the point. Pain tells you that your body's hurt – or, if you've touched scalding water, say, that it's about to be hurt – so you'd better do something. Like, take your hand away now! Or, if you've scraped skin or broken a bone, get help and look after the injury.

Chillies trigger your high-heat damage sensors, making it feel like your mouth's being burned.

NO PAIN

There are rare cases of people born unable to feel pain. This means they can fail to notice injuries. Even really bad ones, which can be deadly without medical help. Their cases show how vital pain is for our health and survival.

Extreme hot and cold

Damaging chemicals

Physical damage

DeTecTing damage

What happens when you feel pain? First, a "damage sensor" in your body is triggered. You have a few different types. They react to: high heat and bitter cold, damaging chemicals (like strong acids), and physical damage (like bashing, squeezing, or crushing). When these sensors are triggered, they send signals to your brain and you feel pain. This nasty sensation makes you pull your body away from the cause immediately, without you having to think about it. This helps you to stay safe and healthy.

The answer?

Not being able to feel pain sounds good, but it would be very bad.

What if you couldn't sweat?

No more damp, sticky PE kit. No more stinging, salty sweat trickling into your eyes. There would be some upsides of not being able to sweat. But if you're thinking there might be some downsides too, you're right. Pretty horrible ones, in fact!

Sweat switch

One of your brain's crucial tasks is to keep your body temperature around 37°C (98.6°F). That's because if it gets much higher – or lower – you could quickly die. When your temperature starts to edge up, your brain presses the "SWEAT!" switch.

On a hot day, or when you're very active, you need to drink EXTRA WATER, as you lose it through sweating.

Mostly water

Sweat is made to order in little glands in the middle layer of your skin. These glands filter your blood to extract water, plus a dash of salt. The sweat then gets squeezed out through tiny tubes onto the surface of your skin.

You have MILLIONS of sweat glands, spread all over your body.

Cool trick

How does sweating cool you down? Heat energy from your body moves into the sweat on your skin. This energy turns the watery sweat into a gas – it makes it "evaporate". The result? Heat has been taken out of your body! Wet skin loses heat a LOT faster than dry skin. If you couldn't sweat, a hot day could quickly lead to "heat exhaustion". People with heat exhaustion can feel faint and sick. If they don't cool down, their condition can worsen into "heatstroke". Someone with heatstroke is no longer able to sweat. Without urgent help, they can fall unconscious and die.

The answer?

Even though your clothes would need less washing, not being able to sweat would be very bad!

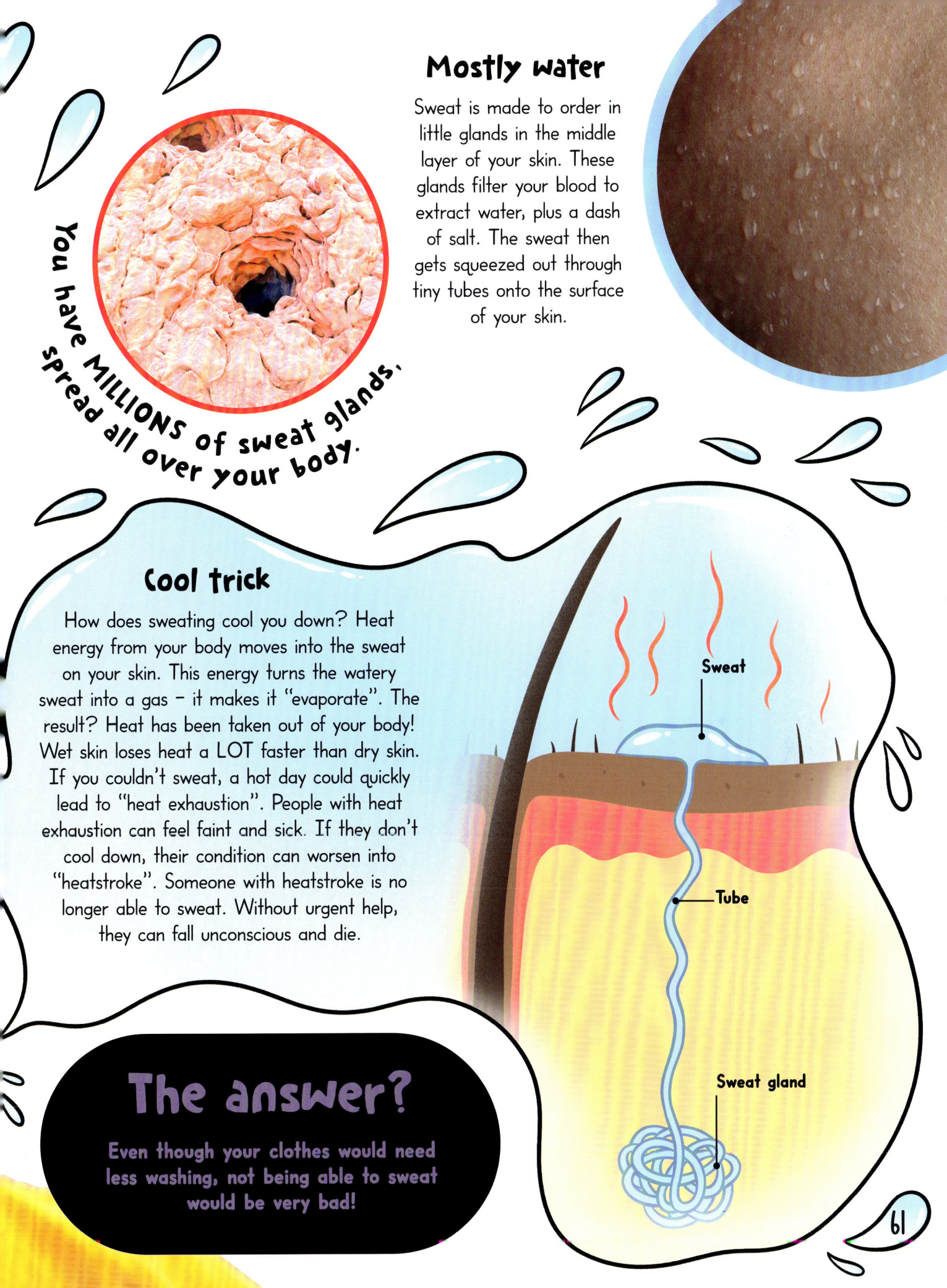

Sweat

Tube

Sweat gland

Night school

It doesn't look like you're up to much while you're asleep. But your brain is actually really busy, working through memories from the day. Sleep helps you to remember facts and get better at new physical tasks. That could be riding a bike, or juggling pears – whatever you like!

What if you never slept?

Doctors say that kids your age should sleep for about 10 hours every night. 10 hours! Just think what you could do with that time if it wasn't spent lying in bed! But what would happen if you did stop sleeping?

Body boost

Regular, undisturbed sleep is good for your heart and your body's ability to fight off germs and heal any wounds. It even helps you to grow. Your body pumps out more "growth hormone" – the chemical that makes you become taller – while you're fast asleep.

Sleep stages

There are four different stages of sleep.
Every night, you move through these stages several times.

Stage 1: You're drifting off to sleep. Or, if it's later in the night, you're only lightly asleep.

Stage 2: A deeper stage of sleep. Important for helping you to remember facts.

Stage 3: Deep sleep. Your brain works at reorganising your memories. You also dream (though they're usually pretty dull dreams).

Stage 4: REM (which stands for "rapid eye movement") sleep. This is when you have wild dreams! REM sleep also helps you to process emotions and get better at physical tasks (like pear juggling).

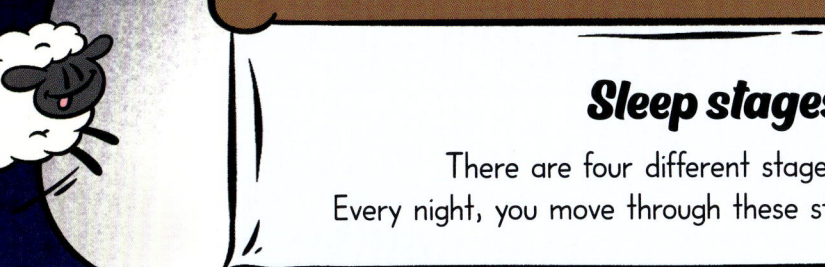

Some animals sleep much longer than humans — koalas sleep up to 20 hours a day!

The answer?

Just one night without sleep would be bad for you. You'd feel extremely tired and struggle to remember things. If you did actually stop sleeping altogether – which would be extremely difficult – scientists think you would die!

What if you refused to get out of bed?

You can read in bed and eat in bed, and you could even do lots of your school work in bed. Plus, if you never left your bed, you couldn't get told off for not making it! But what would happen to your body if you didn't get up again?

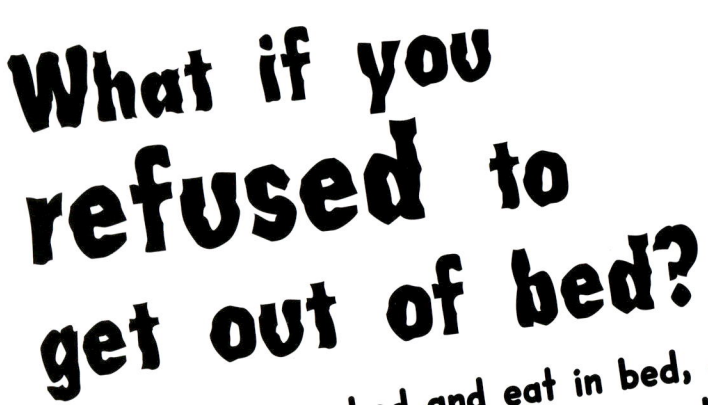

Physical activity is important for your mental health, too.

Wasting muscles

If you don't use the muscles that move your body, they shrink. This happens quickly. After a week of lying in bed, unused muscles can lose up to 40 per cent of their strength! This means you'd quickly feel weaker if you didn't get up and move.

Brittle bones

People have been paid to spend 60 or even 70 days in bed, just so scientists can see what happens to their bodies. This work shows that, as well as muscles, a person's bones get weaker when they don't get up and move, meaning they break more easily.

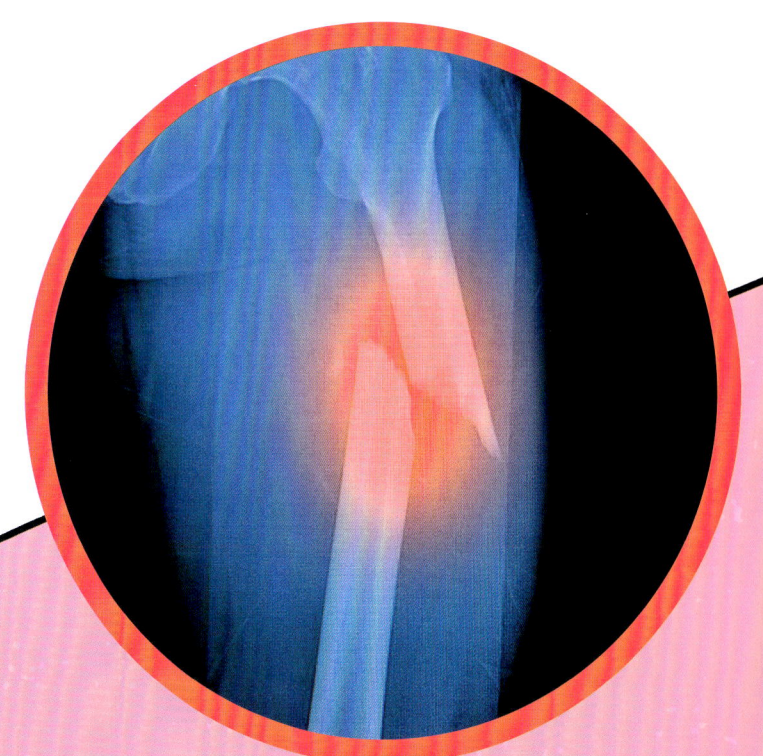

Strengthening exercise

Aerobic exercise

Recommended exercise

To be healthy, kids need to do two types of exercise every week: "aerobic" exercise and "strengthening" exercise. Aerobic exercise gets your heart going and makes you breathe more quickly, like when you run or throw and catch a ball. Strengthening exercise makes your muscles and bones stronger, like when you play football, do gymnastics, or even just jump up and down. Doctors say that kids should aim for an average of one hour of activity every day, which can be moderate or vigorous. "Moderate" means you could still talk while you're exercising — but you couldn't sing!

The answer?

Not only would you get bored staying in bed all the time, it would be bad for your body.

ONE month on

Cells in the top layer of your skin live for about 30 days, and are then replaced. Washing is vital for getting rid of the dead cells. After a month of no washing, you'd see dead skin flakes – like dandruff – on your skin. Plus, there'd be a change in how you smell.

Greasy hair

If you stopped washing your hair, at first it would just become less soft. That would be down to a build-up of dead skin cells at the roots. Then, it would get more and more greasy and matted. After about six months, it might feel as though there's glue in it.

Washing clears away bacteria and mites that live on your skin.

What if you never washed again?

Adults are always going on about having showers and baths. But if you stopped washing, how bad could things get? Well, after about a week, your skin would feel a bit greasy, but you'd be fine. Go for longer without a wash, though, and that would start to change.

Bacteria can grow on your skin if you don't wash.

Sweat **Oil** **Bacteria**

SIX months on

The build up of dead skin would make it harder for your body to lose heat – so you'd feel hotter. Also, skin bacteria, fungi, and mites would probably have grown to such numbers that they would cause skin infections and even open sores. If these bacteria got into your blood, they could cause very serious infections.

SQUEAKY CLEAN
Soap breaks down oils on your skin, making it easier to wash them away. It also removes and kills bacteria and viruses. Try to always wash your hands with soap.

The answer?

Missing the odd shower or bath is not a problem at all. But if you didn't wash for six months, open sores could let harmful bacteria into your body, which would be very bad news.

What if you fell into a cactus patch?

Well, obviously you should get out of that patch as quickly as possible. And probably get help for the cuts and scratches from those terrible, spiky spines. But the good news is, your body's own incredible inbuilt medical team – your "immune system" – will already be on the case.

Cactus spines can be 30 cm (12 in) long!

Vital jobs

Your immune system is dedicated to keeping you healthy. It is made up of specialized cells, chemicals, and some organs – such as your tonsils. It has these crucial jobs:

- It helps keep nasty invaders, like harmful bacteria and viruses, out of your body.
- It attacks and kills any germs that do manage to get in.
- It helps heal any wounds.

React and repair

If you were spiked by a cactus, you would need to make sure no spines had been left in your skin. If they had, they'd need to be pulled out. Then, this would happen:

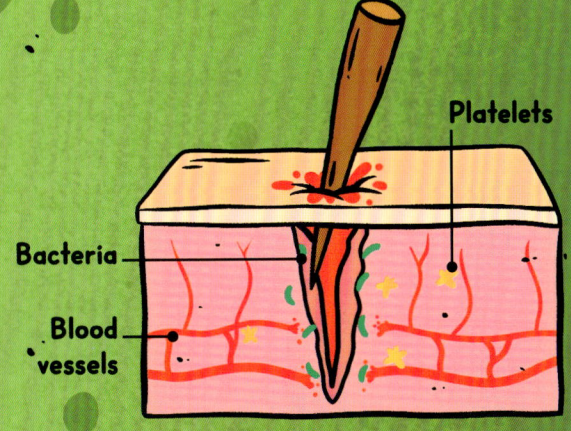

Platelets

Bacteria

Blood vessels

STAGE 1: Blood cells called platelets race to the damaged area and get a scab forming. They also sound the alarm.

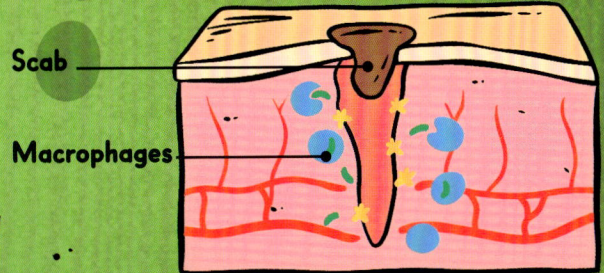

Scab

Macrophages

STAGE 2: Immune cells flood in to attack any harmful bacteria that have come in through the cut. This makes the area swell up and turn red (called inflammation). Cells called "macrophages" gobble up and get rid of bacteria and damaged cells.

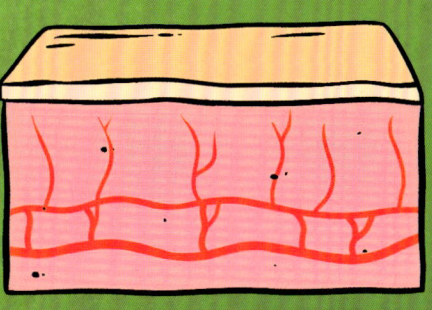

STAGE 3: Finally, the skin grows back to seal up the wound, pushing off the scab. What cactus patch?

Immune boost

To keep your immune system strong, you should: eat nutritious foods, including plenty of fruit and vegetables; get enough sleep and exercise; and also make sure to wash your hands with water and soap before eating and after going to the toilet. That will clean off bacteria and viruses, so give your immune system fewer germs to cope with!

The answer?

Though you might need some help, your immune system will have sprung into action.

Glossary

allergy   when your body reacts strongly to something, such as food, pollen, or animal hair, causing unpleasant symptoms, including itching, sneezing, or difficulty breathing

artery   blood vessel that carries blood away from your heart to all parts of your body

bacteria   tiny living things. Some types can make you ill, but others are helpful and break down food in your gut

bile   yellowish liquid made by your liver that helps your body break down fat in food

blood vessel   tube that carries blood around your body. Arteries, veins, and capillaries are types of blood vessel

bone   one of many hard parts of your body that form your skeleton. Bones help you move and protect your important organs

capillary   tiny blood vessel that carries oxygen and nutrients to your cells and carries waste away from them

carbohydrate   type of nutrient found in foods such as bread and pasta that gives your body energy

carbon dioxide   gas that your cells make as they use up oxygen. You breathe it out of your lungs

cell   smallest part of a living thing. Your cells are the tiny building blocks that make up your body

chemical   one of many substances that can change appearance or combine with other chemicals. Salt, water, and oxygen are all examples of chemicals

fat   type of nutrient found in foods such as butter or nuts that gives your body energy. Stores of fat under your skin also keep you warm

fibre   part of some foods, including fruit and vegetables, that you can't digest

germ   tiny organism, such as a bacterium or virus, that causes illness or infections

gland   small part of your body that makes important substances, such as sweat

haemoglobin   part of red blood cells that carries oxygen

infection   when germs enter your body and make you sick, such as a cold or a sore throat

joint   place where two or more bones meet, such as in your knee, which allows your skeleton to move

keratin   type of protein found in your hair, nails, and skin that makes them tough and healthy

mineral   natural substance, such as calcium or iron, that your body needs to grow and stay strong

muscle   one of many stretchy parts of your body that move your bones and make other organs work

nutrients   important parts of food, such as proteins and vitamins, that help your body grow and stay healthy

organ   special part of your body, such as your heart or lungs, that does an important job to keep you alive

oxygen   gas that you breathe in and that your body needs to make energy

platelet   tiny part of your blood that helps stop bleeding by forming scabs when you get a cut

protein   type of nutrient found in foods such as meat, eggs, and beans that helps to build muscle and repair your body

red blood cell   type of cell that is part of your blood and that carries oxygen to all parts of your body

sugar   type of carbohydrate found in foods such as fruit and chocolate that tastes sweet and gives you quick energy

valve   flap in your heart or veins that makes sure blood flows in the right direction

vein   blood vessel that carries blood back to your heart from your body

virus   tiny germ that can make you ill. Colds and flus are caused by viruses

vitamin   type of nutrient usually found in food, such as vitamin C in oranges and apples, that keeps your body healthy

white blood cell   type of cell that is part of your blood and that fights germs and stops you from getting ill, or helps you to get better when you are ill

Index

ACKNOWLEDGEMENTS

DK | Penguin Random House

Written by Emma Young
Illustrated by Super Freak

Senior editor Olivia Stanford
Project art editor Sonny Flynn
Jacket coordinator Elin Woosnam
Managing art editor Diane Peyton Jones
Production editor Gillian Reid
Senior production controller Inderjit Bhullar
Associate publisher Gemma Farr
Art director Mabel Chan

Consultant Dr Kristina Routh

First published in Great Britain in 2025 by
Dorling Kindersley Limited
20 Vauxhall Bridge Road,
London SW1V 2SA

The authorised representative in the EEA is
Dorling Kindersley Verlag GmbH. Arnulfstr. 124,
80636 Munich, Germany

A CIP catalogue record for this book
is available from the British Library.
ISBN: 978-0-2417-3331-8

Printed and bound in China

www.dk.com

MIX
Paper | Supporting
responsible forestry
FSC™ C018179

This book was made with Forest
Stewardship Council™ certified
paper – one small step in DK's
commitment to a sustainable future.
**Learn more at www.dk.com/uk/
information/sustainability**

For Stelios, Konstantina, Rishan, Romir, and Nina – Emma

DK would like to thank the following people for
their assistance in the preparation of this book:
Charlotte Jennings for design assistance, Kathleen Teece
and Anna Bonnerjea for proofreading, and Carron Brown
for the index.

The publisher would like to thank the following for their kind permission to reproduce their photographs:
(Key: a-above; b-below/bottom; c-centre; f-far; l-left; r-right; t-top)

4 Alamy Stock Photo: Cody Duncan (tl); Hanna Kuprevich (br). **5 Alamy Stock Photo:** Jure Gasparic (tc). **7 Alamy Stock Photo:** Rebecca Smeeth (tr). **8 Getty Images / iStock:** DigitalVision / Sally Anscombe (cb). **9 Shutterstock.com:** Mr.Teerapong Kunkaeo (tc). **10 Alamy Stock Photo:** Meyntjens Jean Paul (cl, tr); Rimom (cra). **11 Adobe Stock:** Artur (tr). **Alamy Stock Photo:** Meyntjens Jean Paul (cr). **12 Dreamstime.com:** Natalia Golovina (crb). **14 Dreamstime.com:** Isselee (b). **15 Dreamstime.com:** Clara Bastian (tr). **16 Alamy Stock Photo:** S.C.Peeps (cb). **Getty Images / iStock:** RusN (l). **16-17 Dreamstime.com:** Sam74100 (bc). **17 Shutterstock.com:** Denklim (tl). **18-19 Dreamstime.com:** Jan Pokorn / Pokec (t). **19 Dreamstime.com:** Anna Komisarenko (tr). **20 Alamy Stock Photo:** Aleksandr Papichev (br). **Getty Images / iStock:** Tom Merton / OJO Images (tc). **22 Alamy Stock Photo:** Blickwinkel / Teigler (c). **23 Adobe Stock:** Deagreez (bl). **Alamy Stock Photo:** Stocktrek Images, Inc. / Todd Winner (tr). **24 Getty Images / iStock:** E+ / ExperienceInteriors (tl). **25 Adobe Stock:** Hjschneider (tc). **Alamy Stock Photo:** Phil Degginger (tr); imageBROKER.com GmbH & Co. KG / Andrey Nekrasov (bl). **26 Shutterstock.com:** Woravit Thongpolyos (cb). **28 123RF.com:** Leonello Calvetti (bl). **Depositphotos Inc:** Rost9 (tl). **31 Alamy Stock Photo:** Stockimo / Megspics (tl). **32 Alamy Stock Photo:** Scenics & Science (tl). **Dreamstime.com:** Prochasson Frederic (cr). **35 Alamy Stock Photo:** RooM the Agency / Darekm101 (tr). **36 Alamy Stock Photo:** Juniors Bildarchiv GmbH / Giel, O. / juniors@wildlife (c). **38 Dreamstime.com:** Diego Vito Cervo (b). **40 Alamy Stock Photo:** Andrey Elkin (r); Zoonar GmbH / Tetiana Troichenko (cb); Tetiana Troichenko (br). **41 Alamy Stock Photo:** Bokehcambodia (clb); imageBROKER.com GmbH & Co. KG / I. Schulz (tl); Zoonar GmbH / Tetiana Troichenko (cla). **42 Alamy Stock Photo:** Andrey Kuzmin (tr). **43 Depositphotos Inc:** Hanohiki (tl). **44 Dreamstime.com:** Rawf88 (cra). **45 Adobe Stock:** Axel Kock (tr). **46 Adobe Stock:** Ulianna19970 (bl). **48 Dreamstime.com:** Sorapop Udomsri (bc). **50 Depositphotos Inc:** Deagreez1 (br). **Shutterstock.com:** Eduardo Menezes (tr). **51 Alamy Stock Photo:** Rick & Nora Bowers (tr). **52-53 123RF.com:** Fotomaximum (bc). **53 Alamy Stock Photo:** Tim Gainey (tl). **54 Alamy Stock Photo:** Lisa de Araujo Food Photography (tc). **Dreamstime.com:** Lars Christensen (bl). **57 Adobe Stock:** HalynaRom (clb). **58 123RF.com:** Tatiana Popova / Violin (ca). **Shutterstock.com:** Gravicapa (tl). **59 Shutterstock.com:** Photo-Art Jo (tl). **60-61 Getty Images / iStock:** Moment / Anna Cinaroglu (bc). **61 Depositphotos Inc:** Animaxx3d (tl). **Shutterstock.com:** Piboon Chiantanrak (tr). **62 Getty Images / iStock:** E+ / Hispanolistic (tl). **62-63 Depositphotos Inc:** Nordseegold (bc). **64 Getty Images / iStock:** PeakSTOCK (tr). **65 Adobe Stock:** Praisaeng (tr). **66 Dreamstime.com:** Mariia Boiko (tr). **Science Photo Library:** Power and Syred (cl). **68 123RF.com:** Alfio Scisetti (l). **69 Dreamstime.com:** Serg_Velusceac (tr)

All other images © Dorling Kindersley Limited.